Legends

of the

Star Ancestors

Legends
of the
Star Ancestors

Stories of
Extraterrestrial Contact
from Wisdomkeepers
around the World

AS SPOKEN TO

Nancy Red Star

BEAR & COMPANY
ROCHESTER, VERMONT

Bear & Company
One Park Street
Rochester, Vermont 05767
www.InnerTraditions.com

Bear & Company is a division of Inner Traditions International

LIBRARY OF CONGRESS CATALOGING-IN-PUBLICATION DATA
Legends of the star ancestors : stories of extraterrestrial contact from
wisdomkeepers around the world / as spoken to Nancy Red Star.
    p. cm.
  ISBN 1-879181-79-7
  1. Human-alien encounters. I. Red Star, Nancy, 1950-
  BF2050 .L44 2002
  001.942—dc21
                                  2002005005

Printed and bound in the United States at Lake Book Manufacturing, Inc.

10   9   8   7   6   5   4   3   2   1

Text design by Peri Champine, layout by Priscilla Baker
This book was typeset in Sabon with Papyrus and Stone Sans as the display
typefaces

To all sentient beings who walk
the Path of Purification

Contents

Acknowledgments

Thanks to:

My beloved mother, Joyce Burroughs Matthews, and my great-grandfathers, Joseph Matthews and John Burroughs.

All the Elders, young and old, who assisted me with interviews, love, and support, especially the late Mali Keating, the late Troy Lang of the International Treaty Council and Chief of the Abenaki Nation of Missisquoi, and the Odanak Family Band.

My literary agent, William Gladstone, his family, and everyone at Waterside Productions, including Nancy Aceuido.

My editors at Inner Traditions, especially Lee Awbrey.

Allison Rae, who assisted me in creating a beautiful manuscript.

All who generously assisted me in the completion of my manuscript, including Naoko Hitomi, the Daniel M. Salter Library, Dreamtime Gallery, Elaine La Foret, Dorit Bat Shalom, The Aquarian Mission, James Lujan and Taos Communications, Mary Decarr and Wings, and the Dharma Triyana Monastery.

All the artists who contributed their work.

Photoworks Lab and Camera Darkroom, for printing my photographs.

Finally, many thanks to Chief Homer St. Francis and my family at the Sovereign Abenaki Nation of Missisquoi.

Foreword

The Wisdom that Binds Us

"The roots of all living things are tied together. When a mighty tree is felled, a star falls from the sky; before you cut down a mahogany you should ask permission of the keeper of the forest, and you should ask permission of the keeper of the star. A star falls from the sky; before you cut down a mahogany you should ask permission of the keeper of the forest and you should ask permission of the keeper of the star . . . Ask . . . permission . . . star . . . permission . . . star. Star."

CHAN KIN VIEJO,
LACANDONE T'O'OHIL (THE GREAT ONE), FROM
The Last Lords of Palenque

Chan Kin Viejo was speaking from experience when he told us of the interconnection that not only binds us and is everywhere around us, but ultimately is us. We are not separate from nature; we are a part of nature.

One need only mention Chan Kin Viejo's name and the almond-shaped eyes of the Hach Winik Maya light up with joyful remembrances. Kin Paniagua recounts how Chan Kin Viejo, his father-in-law, was a jovial man who saw the interconnectedness of all things and the flow of all moments. He was happy to play his rattle and sing songs, odes to the jungle that he himself had composed. He was a bearer of light for his people until his last days. Sensing his death, Chan Kin Viejo made one last trip to the sacred temples of Yaxchilan in the jungles of Chiapas, Mexico. One last time he negotiated the steep incline that leads to the temple of the First Father. Solemnly, he entered the ancient abode of his ancestors, singing and praying softly in the words of those who shone the light long ago and who had passed the torch down the succeeding generations of light-bearing t'o'ohils. Gracefully holding a piece of "pom," the sacred copal resin, he offered the sweet smoke of the tree sap to his ancestors. Chan Kin Viejo left the world shortly after. His physical body is gone but his spirit lives on in his family, his people, and his words as well as actions.

Chan Kin Viejo was a t'o'ohil, a light-bearer. He was part of a lineage that extends beyond the old Mayan empire. The third book of the Popol Vuh speaks of the t'o'ohil bearing the light that led his people to safety after they fled their sinking homeland. This migration was of paramount importance to the t'o'ohil and his people. They were bearers of wisdom, storehouses of ancient ways. Eventually they would find a home under the shadows of the great sacred "Witz" mountain. Their settlement grew into a great empire, and the knowledge they had carried there became the backbone of the great Mayan empire. Just as the t'o'ohil thousands of years ago, Chan Kin Viejo was a light unto himself and therefore his people as well. And just as Chan Kin Viejo was a fountain of ancient wisdom, so exist many keepers of truth who are part of an eternal unbroken chain of wisdom that have long awaited the time in which the old ways could be openly discussed. Those times appear to have arrived.

While Star Ancestors have been all around the globe collecting wisdom for new eyes to feast upon, a common thread has become evident in the teachings as well as the actions, the lifestyles of those people involved. Be it Japan, Tibet, Australia, Cuba, Israel, the jungles of Mexico, Peru, Colombia, or the sacred mesas of the Hopi, the truth complements and extends itself in all directions. Those who visit us from the skies are not "aliens" any more than we are. They have always been around; history overflows with records of their existence. Our world is on the brink of a new paradigm of experience. We stand challenged to modify not only our actions but our way of thinking as well. We must take literally the words for so long seen as myth. We cannot go on without the support of the life system that is all around us, within us. The trees are not there for the taking, the oceans are not garbage dumps, and our air is not a negotiable commodity.

Many of us have a strange feeling that things are not the way they should be. Something seems to be off. How many of us could accept the truth if it were presented to us in a manner we could comprehend? What if most of what you have been taught is fiction? What if you are part of something much larger than you ever dreamed of? Is it not worth the chance? Can we suspend judgment long enough to take a real glimpse at what is out there?

Listen to the words that have traveled through time and space to reach you today. . . . Look to the skies and look within yourself and realize that they are one and the same place. . . . Ask permission of the keepers of the forest, ask permission of the keepers of the stars. . . .

PAUL WERNER DUARTE,
German-Mayan Anthropologist

In the beginning, according to many creation stories, the four races sat in a circle on Mother Earth. Each race was told by the Creator and the guardian Star People about their individual responsibilities and their roles in the sacred hoop of life. The teachings were divided into four equal parts and one was given to each color. The four root races were then sent to the four directions of Mother Earth and each was given a special knowledge of creation. The Yellow People were entrusted with Spirit and the element of Fire. The Black/Brown People were given Soul corresponding to the element of Water. The White People learned about the Mind and the element of Air. The Red People had the Body and the element of Earth. Each race was given only a quarter of the whole truth of Creation. *Legends of the Star Ancestors* mends the hoop of all races by bringing into balance the original teachings and knowledge of the sky heroes.

Introduction

The Time of Purification

"The sky heroes of the Dreamtime made every-thing and everything was made for a reason. They act as our guides in the Dreamtime. We believe that all life is part of one universal whole, an indivisible unity that can be traced back to the great spirit ancestors, when the world was still formless, they came from the Earth and the sky, wandered the land, creating all things. In ritual when we sing and dance, we create the old stories. These ancestors are still with us—part of us as we are part of them. Together, we join them, in the Dreamtime. . . a time before any man walked the earth."

KARIDJI, WURUNJERI TRIBE,
AUSTRALIAN ABORIGINE

Mayan Elder Danceta Conchero

Keepers around the world have seen signs occurring, signs that were predicted by ancient prophecies. These signs show the Time Keepers that they must speak their closely held knowledge regarding our origin from the Star Nations; the influence of visitation on the formation of culture, traditions, and ceremony; and the imminent return of our Star Ancestors. Our history with extraterrestrial life is of global significance at this time.

The Purification, the Earth changes, the cleansing, the Tribulation is the time when humanity will choose the way of Peace or the Path of Destruction, the spiritual life or the way of war. We are living in this period called the Time of Purification. It is during this time that we have the power to change our destiny. A chance to choose. If humanity ignores the prayers, we will continue to see the Earth changes, the floods, droughts, earthquakes, tornadoes, hailstorms, famine, and disease.

Nature, the original peoples, and the spirit of the Ancestors are giving us warnings and revealing the ancient secrets of balance and survival. Some do not choose to listen; they are not hearing the message. Those who do are preparing for the construction of another world. But any and all who seek a new world are welcome to learn and change from the knowledge provided within the prophecies emerging from around the globe. In *Star Ancestors* and *Legends of the Star Ancestors* all the colors will speak and we will not only listen but also see. We will learn that unless we heed the warnings, our planet will continue to purge its surface in order to preserve itself. We are together looking beyond ourselves, past Earth, into the cosmos, to create a zone of mercy between all the races of this world and other worlds. We become citizens of the universe. We grow up, inviting all humanity to realize their Star Ancestry in the wonder-struck awakening of our collective genetic memories. The relationship continues upon a spiritual odyssey, a path for the sunbow walking, wherever we may be. As the gateways open, we carry the light.

The Tibetans are a necessary link in ensuring the development of humankind's spiritual nature. The Hopi Prophecy talks about the Red Hat, Red Cloak People who come from the East to North America to bring wisdom and knowledge. The people are encouraged to accept and understand these teachings, and to put them next to their own. The prophecy warns that if these teachings are not used to guide the people back to the spiritual path, then the Red Hat, Red Cloak People will come from the West. They could come in large numbers, and they could fall out of the sky and overtake the land in one day, just like red ants. They would have no mercy for anyone. The Hopi are instructed to hide if this comes to pass.

As we align with the cosmic laws, we awaken to the unifying theme of our own evolution, with one voice, a procession of faith, fires to light the way for the Creator. All the colors hold knowledge; now, in a good way, we must share the Teaching. For only if we do will we be able to accept colors from other realms.

1 The World Peace

Compassionate Enlightenment

KHENPO KHARTHUR RINPOCHE
Tibetan Buddhist Monk

> "A mountain castle opened its gates for the
> eagles of Divine Guidance—a meeting place, a
> refuge of angels who, by their loving kindness,
> return to Earth dimension in times of strife and
> confusion. The mountain is called Great
> Patience. . . ."
>
> TIBETAN PROVERB

KHENPO KHARTHUR RINPOCHE

Khenpo Kharthur Rinpoche was born in Tibet and came to America in exile twenty-five years ago. He is the head abbot of the Dharma Triyana Chakra Monastery in Woodstock, New York. His monastery is the Seat of the Karmpa in the West (karmpa means "enlightenment"). Since his arrival, Khenpo Kharthur Rinpoche has helped create forty-two branch centers to teach and explain the dharma—the lawful order of the universe.

I am very happy that you have come here to the monastery to meet with me and talk about dharma and the World Peace. In the Tibetan tradition, the high-flying bird—the hawk—which you saw circling above the monastery, is also a very good sign.

I came to the United States twenty-two years ago. People at that time did not seem to know very much about Buddhism. We Tibetans realized that it would be beneficial to teach and explain the dharma. We began to talk to people about how to create peace within their heart and peace within the world. We taught how to move beyond suffering. I have been doing that for these twenty-two years. We now have this monastery and forty-two branch centers. If you look at me you will see what I do.

In our tradition, to understand karma we must first look at our present lives. If we are living a happy life and things are going well for us, we can draw the conclusion that we were involved in positive actions in our previous lives. If our lives are not going so well, it is a sign that we engaged in negative actions in the past. If you have the seed of a medicinal flower and you plant this seed, the medicinal flower will grow. If you don't harvest the seed that flower produces, then there is nothing to be born again. So karma is like planting a seed for what will arise in the future. Karma that we have accumulated in the past is something we experience now. Future karma is something that is open to change—that we can change now by our present actions. If we have a bad situation in our life, through the proper kind of motivation and a heartfelt good intention, we can change that situation to a good one.

Karma is not carved in stone. Our own actions can transform our lives. Much of this depends on the individual and his or her motivation. There are some individuals who have a wonderful altruism. They are called *bodhisattvas* in our tradition. Their whole being is dedicated toward benefiting others. To do this they first work on themselves. Their own mind becomes enlightened and realized. Then they are able to vastly benefit other sentient beings. If people don't first work on themselves, if they don't develop their own positive qualities, they will have nothing to give humanity. When they haven't developed themselves, their potential is less. How beneficial an individual is to the planet depends on his or her own spiritual development.

In our Tibetan culture, there are many different ways of healing. There are herbal medicines like moxa bustin, and so on. However, the heart of the tradition is prayer. Prayer creates the healing. When a Lama who is making a prayer for an unwell person is a true practitioner, he has developed qualities on the path of his practice, and the person who is receiving the prayer has faith in the healing. In this situation the prayer can be very effective. If the Lama hasn't developed the qualities necessary for healing, however, then when he offers the prayer he is just repeating words, and the person receiving the prayer is not sure if anything is happening. In this situation it is very difficult for the healing prayer to work.

Mainly, for us Tibetans, it is taught that the root of all illness is in the mind. In order to relieve oneself of the suffering the mind can go through, one has to look into the nature of the mind. Illness comes from an imbalance with the elements—the four elements. These are Earth, Water, Fire, and Air. There is a correspondence between inner and outer elements and the outside and inside of the body. The way illness comes about is through the imbalance of the inner and outer elements. In our tradition, anger is considered the most negative emotion you can have. The way to deal with this emotion is to develop patience. Patience is the antidote to anger. It works in this way: If somebody hurts you, then you would reflect upon that person's situation—how that sentient being is suffering with the burden of all the hatred he or she is carrying. This burden of anger-turned-hatred has brought illness. Instead of reflecting on yourself, you reflect on the suffering of this human being, which brings about compassion.

To deal with the emotion of fear, you have to see where it comes from. You must look into the fear, asking, "What is it?" By looking, we can see which conditions create fear. Sometimes it is very difficult to look and see this emotion directly. First comes recognition, then

ཨོཾ	OM	Enlightened Body
ཨཱཿ	AH	Enlightened Speech
ཧཱུྃ	HUNG	Enlightened Mind
ཧོ	HO	Enlightened Activity

OHIO. *For the Shawnee, the word Ohio means "Place of Beginning."
The Tibetan people also have a word Ohio that means "The Dharma
Teachings," and, when spelled out, appears as shown above.*

comes understanding. Fear is different for different people. For some,
fear comes from not having enough food. For others, it might come
from not having friends or from sitting alone with no husband, wife,
or relatives. It might come from natural disasters such as the floods
we have seen in the south or the winds and tornadoes we have had
here. There are many different causes for fear, so one must look to
understand the conditions that bring it about. Then, very slowly,
through doing a dharma practice, through developing the wish to
benefit other beings, the fear will diminish. There are practices in
Tibetan Buddhism called *shinay,* which means freeing the mind
through peace. By bringing the mind to tranquillity while engaging
in this practice, we will free the mind from fear.

There are two aspects to suffering—one positive, one negative.
The negative side is that your mind becomes disturbed from the suffering and you increase your negative emotions. When that happens,
you might do something negative to other people. The suffering may

be a cause for creating more suffering. The positive side is that the suffering can wake you up; it can encourage you to look at your situation and change it. You can say, "I'm suffering because of the things that I myself have done." Then you take responsibility, which leads to change. Suffering can be a very good tool for lessening pride and arrogance. Sometimes individuals are proud and think they control their world. Suffering comes along and makes them ordinary, brings them down to the level of ordinary people. If they can see that they are suffering because of their own negative actions, then they can change.

There exists a connection between the anger and the fear within the sentient being's mind and the natural disasters we are now experiencing on the planet; these emotions create an imbalance that is then reflected in nature. There is a very strong correlation between the planets and stars and the inner body, an essential relationship between the outer and inner worlds. In order to create peace on this planet, it is not enough to just do rituals, bang a drum, and blow horns. We must turn around and look inside our own mind to see how it works, how it operates. Some minds have more positive qualities, while some have more negative. According to the Buddhist tradition, in order to increase the positive qualities in our mind, we engage in authentic spiritual practices. These are the meditative practices that lead us to an understanding of the nature of the mind and how to develop positive qualities. The practice also teaches us about the negative qualities of the mind that lead us toward suffering. These negative aspects can develop strongly enough to manifest in the outside world. They come into the outside world as wars, disputes, and fighting. The origin of all the problems we have in the outer world is within our minds. That is why the first action we do to create world peace is to go within.

When people become enlightened, they don't just cringe back in their chair and do nothing. Since enlightenment has the essence of compassion, they move out into the world. For example, the Buddha became enlightened two thousand years ago, and he did not just stay sitting under a tree. He moved out into the world and taught. He

DHARMA TRIYANA CHAKRA MONASTERY

shared his views of meditation and his realization with other beings. If you put a small light to dry grass, it will create a flame and blaze. This is what happens when one person becomes enlightened—he or she goes out in the world to spread the light around.

There is one thing which we are doing at the Dharma Triyana Chakra Monastery. For the Year 2000 we participated in a practice called Amieabha, or Buddha of Infinite Light. Before the New Year came, we lit lights at all the centers around the world, beginning with Siberia and New Zealand. We offered lights at the beginning of New Year's Day and as the dawn broke around the planet, we made prayers for peace and happiness for the next thousand years. We were thinking of a very long-term basis with the dedication of this world-wide practice. With the lights being originally lit all around the planet, world peace will grow.

In Tibetan tradition there is no contradiction between the spiritual path and technology. Think of the ocean as an ocean of suffering. If you were to cross over that ocean, you would need some skillful means to do that—you would need a boat, then the human being can ride on the boat to cross the ocean's suffering. For me, technology is that boat, a skillful means to help us go beyond suffering. Technology can be useful on the path; the outcome depends on the intention of the person using the technology.

The essence of the dharma is to benefit all sentient beings as we open our hearts to compassion. We call the earth Mother. In our Tibetan understanding, there are deities that belong to the elements—Water, Earth, Fire, and Air. Here at the monastery there are deities belonging to the trees in the woods. When the sixteenth Karmapa (*karmapa* means an incarnation of an enlightened mind) was here, he blessed the land. He took one of these local resident spirits and made it the protector for this place. The protector's name is The Golden One. We give offerings to this protector every day as part of our way of connecting with the local spirits.

There are also spirits belonging to the sky, called Dakinis. *Dakini* translates as "sky goer," those who move through the sky. That is only a very superficial understanding because the Sky Goers truly benefit sentient beings. Their whole motivation is to benefit humanity. There are two classes of Sky Goers: Wisdom Dakinis and Worldly Dakinis. Through an authentic practice of meditation and prayer, we connect our inner body with the stars; the Sky Goers are there for the benefit of humanity and to guide the next thousand years toward World Peace.

The essence of the dharma is to benefit all sentient beings as we open our hearts to our Mother Earth from the beautiful Red Indian tradition.

Compassionate Enlightenment

The Red Hat   Red Cloak People   Who Carry

The Teachings   Of Compassionate Enlightenment

A Meditation   Of Prayerful Wisdom

Sky Goers   Ancient Ancestors   Guardians

The Wisdom Dakinis   The Worldly Dakinis

Of Our Earth   The Dharma   Of the Land

Returns   To the Red Man   And   The Golden One

Offerings   For Our Protectors   Who Move

Through the Sky   For the Benefit

Of Sentient Beings   Prepare   An Altar

For Body-Mind-Spirit   An Essence

An Authentic   Practice

The Healing   The World Peace   The Essence

Incarnate   To Benefit   All Humanity   In   A Time

Of Strife   And Confusion   The Bodhisattvas

Of Realization

Women hold the responsibility of nurturing and protecting the cycles. When we pass into the next world, women return as the true culture bearers of fertility and rebirth—holding the seeds as Ambassadors of Wisdom, challenged by a world of patriarchy crumbling at our feet. As an equal with man, woman will rise above him to assume her rightful place as woman is renewed again.

The female species on planet Earth have a deeper understanding of the balance intrinsic to nature, and with this knowledge women hold and nurture the process of an emerging world. The power to give birth and regenerate creation is women's source of strength and leadership.

2

A Spiritual Renewal

The Big Mother

Rabbi Ohad Ezrah
Israeli Scholar and Spiritual Leader

"I give you the end
of the golden string,
Only, wind it into a ball,
It will lead you
In at heaven's gate
Built in Jerusalem's wall."

William Blake, Poet, *Jerusalem*

RABBI OHAD EZRAH

Rabbi Ohad Ezrah is the director of Ha'makom [in English, "the place and the space"] and codirector of MINAD [in English, the Institute for Spirituality and Jewish Renewal]. Ha'makom is the first non-Orthodox institution to integrate prayer and spiritual studies with meditation, music, dance, and yoga. Rabbi Ezrah has created a new indigenous cultural renaissance by blending Jewish mysticism with the Eastern Orthodox wisdom.

Rabbi Ezrah was raised in a secular family and began his spiritual quest at the age of fifteen, traveling to India and Japan, where he became a Zen Buddhist monk. Now thirty-seven, he is a husband and father, an accomplished academic scholar, and the author of three books. His words are encouragement for the mind-body-spirit.

I am of the tradition of Chasidic rabbis, who are somewhat like shamans. I myself do not perform ceremonies, however; I am a teacher and a spiritual leader. I came to the United States to teach and write on feminine ecology, the Gaia concept in the Kabbalah, at the University of Oregon.

Some years ago I felt the need to establish a new concept of a place of study. This new place would concentrate on the spiritual philosophy of Judaism and on meditation to open the heart and to blend with the spiritual sources of the Kabbalah through Chasidism. Chasidism is a way of understanding the wisdom of the Kabbalah that is more connected to the soul and to psychology—that is, that focuses on personal growth. You can understand the Kabbalah on different levels. It is, however, the secret spiritual and mystical part of our Jewish wisdom. In Jewish wisdom, you have the rules or the laws which are called "Halacha" and contain the deep philosophy. Then you have the spiritual and mystical components which are considered the secret part of Jewish wisdom called the Kabbalah. Literally translated, *kabbalah* means "oral tradition." This is the accepted tradition of the oral transmission of knowledge; you literally receive the teaching from the Kabbalah. An example I usually give is that to learn the Kabbalah is to know the map of Jerusalem.

Chasidic rabbis are spiritual healers—sometimes of the body, but most importantly of the community. Our work involves mainly energy healing and balancing or helping people. We are here for the people; we don't look for a reward. There is a feminine equivalent to a rabbi, who goes by the same name. In the past, only rarely was there a woman ordained to this sect. There was a woman who was the daughter of the Baal Shem Tov who was the first master of our tradition. This literally means "owner of the good name." His daughter Odel was acting as a spiritual leader of this tradition. She performed miracles and she was like a shaman. People came to her for blessings, and to teach them knowledge even though she did not have the title of rabbi. The rabbis came to her to have blessings; she was more than a rabbi, who is like a Ph.D. Even if you have a Ph.D., it doesn't say that you are a great teacher or a great scholar. It is a title. A large part of our greatest master teachers had no titles, just a name.

From time to time, I run into controversy with the keepers of the old traditions—or the ones who think they are. I think they are not. I studied with them for many, many years. I was part of their world, but then I came to the conclusion that it was not completely right. It was archaic, and instead we have to look toward the future and a spiritual renewal. I met Rabbi Zalman Schakter-Shalomi, who is best known as the father of the Jewish Renewal movement. I realized that I wanted to change Israeli society. I was ordained and became a rabbi outside the borders.

The name of our spiritual center is Ha'makom (pronounced *ham-ma-kum*), which in Hebrew means "the place and the space." It is situated on the cliffs of the Judean desert. Ha'makom offers sunrise yoga, tai chi, prayer, and meditation. Afternoons are devoted to text study, in which the focus is on mystical and Chasidic teachings. Teachers from a variety of spiritual traditions are invited to lecture. As a Jewish retreat and spiritual learning center, Ha'makom lies on the cutting edge of a recent phenomenon—increasing numbers of secular Israelis want to access Jewish sources and tradition, but not within an Orthodox framework. Many of these Israelis discovered a personal interest in spiritual teachings during travels to India and the Far East. Upon returning to their own country, they no longer viewed Judaism as the sole domain of Orthodox Jews and the traditional yeshiva system. That is why we chose the name Ha'makom; it implies giving space for people to be whatever they are on their path.

Ha'makom is a pilot center. We hope someday to expand to a beautiful location we have found near the Dead Sea. The Dead Sea

WISDOMKEEPER
by Dorit Bat Shalom

and the Dead Sea scrolls, ancient Hebrew scriptures, were found hidden in caves in this region.

In our wisdom, talking about star beings that appear from outer space is somehow not considered totally exciting. Obviously, we have many, many beings in the outer dimensions and they are here all the time. There are a multitude of these entities, whether they live here, in another dimension, or on another planet. In Jewish mysticism it is not exciting for us because we just know that they exist. Out there or here—it is the same for us. I don't care whether they have wings or appear in disks or spaceships. If you are spiritual and it is important for you, they will appear and teach you. But we don't assume each spiritual entity is a good teacher.

Imagine if we, as human beings, were to appear on another planet—as astronauts, perhaps—and start to teach. Maybe we would have some correct knowledge in our teachings, or maybe our teachings would not be correct knowledge. In Hebrew we have different words for "angels"—spiritual entities that do not have a body. If they want to wear a body, they can, whether it is a body of fire, of an animal, or of anything. They are more spiritual than humans and can give us information, but we have to be cautious, because like humans, angels are creatures. Like all creatures, their knowledge is limited to their own experience.

Humans have seen entities through all of our existence. They wear a body, and they come down to the physical world. If angels came with masks and tunics in the times of the Romans, so too could they appear as "ETs" today. They can wear a body and they can come down to the physical world. In Biblical times they were carried on horses; today they have UFOs. I have, myself, with my wife, seen a UFO—a craft of a kind that I had never seen or heard of—about 200 meters from our house. I have also had all kinds of experiences with spirit teachers that came down to the physical world. But it's important not to forget that all of us, all entities—the humans, the spirits, the angels, the extraterrestrials—are creatures, and we have to look above to connect with the Great

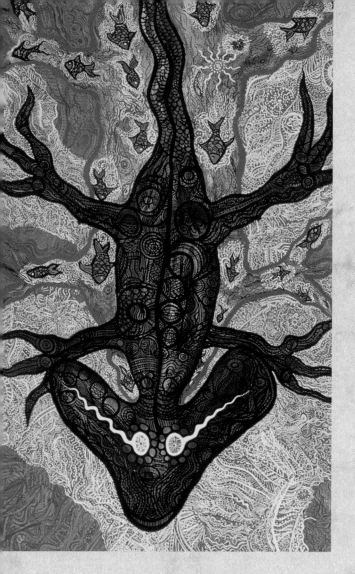

Previous page:
Blue Sky Woman
by Colleen Kelly

Left:
Sea Serpent
by Jingalu

Below:
Land of Enchantment
by Mitch Gyson

Opposite:
Machu Pichu
photograph by Luis E. Mejia
Kogi
photograph by Luis E. Mejia
Rainbow
photograph by Hiroshi Haga
Santería
photograph courtesy of Ana Brito

Overleaf (left and right pages):
The Arrival
by Lorne Kris Honyumptewa

Left:
Sky People
by Jerome Water Eagle

Below:
Forestland
by Jingalu

Opposite (top):
Dessert Dweller
by Dorit Bat Shalom

Opposite (bottom left):
**Woman Who Weaves
the World**
by Desiree Fitzgibbon

Opposite (bottom right):
Hope
by Jingalu

Overleaf:
First Vision
by Jerome Water Eagle

Mystery we call God. This is infinity, and we are not supposed to be stuck in the middle. We are all the creation of Spirit, and we must open our hearts to the infinity. Then we can see that, yes, we have special teachings available to us from extraterrestrials, from people, from angels, from UFOs, even from animals. All can find the teachings whenever they come.

In our tradition, we have stories like in the beginning of the Bible, in Genesis. There were the Bnai, the Sons of God—Bnai Elohim. These are the men who fell from heaven and married the women, the daughters of Man. They became giants, a generation of giants. This you will find in the beginning of Genesis. In our tradition we see them as the Sons of God, as a kind of species of angel. Again, we have many, many species of angels. In Hebrew there are names for hundreds of species of angels, demons, and spiritual entities surrounding us all the time. At this time in the Bible, during Genesis, they came down in a physical body and blended with mankind. Yes, we were seeded in this instance, by a star seed. But Earth is a star also. Do we really care if we came from this star or another star? No. There is nothing to hide with star seed knowledge.

In his book *Paradigm Shift*, Rabbi Zalman Schakter-Shalomi speaks of the transformation foretold by Shmi Tot. At this time, on the planet we find ourselves in not so good a situation. We have this tradition called Shmi Tot. According to this tradition, the world exists in cycles of seven thousand years. Each cycle ends in some kind of transformation, a disaster that ends the world as we know it and begins a new cycle and a new world. According to the Hebraic calendar, we are now 5,761 years into the current cycle and we find ourselves and our planet in not so good a situation. The seven thousandth year is the shift time. Within the Hebrew tradition there will be some kind of end of our world and transition into the next cycle. This transition is not just about disaster—it is a good renewal from one cycle to another. But the last thousand years, which we are close to, is considered the cleansing period. It will not happen in our time but perhaps in the time of our grandsons and granddaughters.

What is important now is how we see the world. We see our main role as being connected to the Creator. The Creator has created all the entities. In Hebrew, we don't have a gender-free name for the Creator, and we don't use the pronoun "it." We can call the Creator He or She or whatever we like. We cannot connect directly with infinity so these words *He* or *She* place a limited concept on that which we call God. The Great Mystery is above any concept. To humans, the Great Mystery can appear as a wise old man, a very beautiful sexy woman, a fire, or the sound of silence. With figures, without figures—this concept of God is above everything. The important question is: What is the relevance of the concept of God to us, for our spiritual growth? What is important is holding sparks of divinity.

Everywhere—in the physical world, in the spiritual world, in the souls—there is divinity. Everywhere. And we have to reveal this divinity and take the sparks, returning them to the holy fire. The beginning of the world was like the breaking of the vessel of holy fire. This is a symbol: the vessel was filled with light, and the light was so strong and powerful that the vessel was broken. The world is based on the broken vessel and the sparks of light spread all over the world. Kabbalastic work is mainly to connect with the sparks. When a Kabbalist goes into the world he always looks for the sparks of divinity. We go to the world, we go to the people, but inside we are always looking for the sparks of divinity. There are sparks of divinity within each Shmi Tot cycle as well, so we care for the cycle. We are located here and now, so we have to work here and now.

The lost civilization of Atlantis may be parallel to a previous Shmi Tot cycle—a cycle wherein there was a world filled with great wisdom, and great knowledge. Before the seven cycles we are in now, there were seven cycles of a more spiritual nature—a higher level. Now, however, it is like we have been going downward and

HEBRAIC SYMBOLS
by Dorit Bat Shalom

our role as spiritual people is to work with the body and the physical world. So Jewish wisdom is to not escape from the body; we are not monks in a monastery. You cannot be a rabbi, usually, unless you are married, because we want spirituality to go into the world.

For hundreds of years wisdom has been out of balance. All the world—the Jews, the Buddhists, the Christians, the Native Americans, and almost every other tradition—has been patriarchal. The women remained on the side, where they had a role. In Judaism, women had a very important role. They were never considered an instrument that husbands owned. We don't have this concept. Marriage was not created to bind the woman; she was always a person in her own right. She had her role as caretaker, like the wings of the family and the cycle. The masculine symbolizes going outside; the man is hunting for knowledge, for food, for money. Man is also hunting the sparks of spirituality, in and out, going in and out of the world. The feminine is a symbol of the cycle, and women are protectors of the cycle. This is very important and very holy in our tradition.

The Kabbalah is all about eroticism; like Tantra, it is all about the spiritual connections to the physical. In the Jewish Temple— which I consider to be the original source of knowledge—we had a sanctuary known as the Holy of the Holiest. It was a temple and then, inside the temple, through a yard and entrance hall, there was a shrine which was cloaked. What was inside, underneath, were two cherubs, two angels with wings made out of gold, and they were having sex together. One was female and the other was male and they were making love. And this is in the Holy of the Holiest. As the two angels making love they covered the Ten Commandments. If you took those two statues of gold and put them in a synagogue today you would be kicked out immediately. So where is the balance today? The indigenous tradition of Israel was about the holiness of eroticism. All the patterns on the walls of the Temple depicted the male and the female making love, so that when you entered the Jewish Temple you were surrounded by erotic images.

These images were the symbol of the unification of the people and the divine. Within the erotic is the balance that symbolizes many concepts that are the core of Kabbalah. We are always remaking unification—this is the spark. We learn how to make the revelation of this spark to unite it again through some kind of sexual unification in spirit.

I am cautious to conclude that the seed of this spark was created by races from other realms. I have it in the back of my mind, but I don't jump to conclusions. Until I see evidence, I see it only as a possibility. The guardians, the spiritual entities which are considered as gods or deities in other cultures, we see as spiritual creatures of the Creator.

It is written in the Kabbalah that there are many, many worlds. Not only four worlds that are known, but thousands of dimensions and worlds which surround us. The concept of Earth as feminine and as a living being is written in the Kabbalah.

The awakening of this feminine nature, which we are seeing now, is written in the Kabbalah. Sixteenth-century Lurianic codes prophesied the feminist movement of the twentieth and twenty-first centuries and the awakening of the feminine nature. According to Lurianic Kabbalah, in the beginning, women were very small and under control of the masculine. Now is the time when the feminine will be divided from the masculine to develop until she becomes equal, totally equal, to the male, the masculine. Only when she is totally equal to the masculine will the male and female turn face to face.

Imagine a male and a female standing back to back, just touching. They don't have any deep connection, only a functional connection. Back-to-back is a symbol of function. Then they separate, and the female starts to grow and develop herself. She is getting energy, but not in the same way as when they were connected. When they were connected her spiritual nourishment came from the masculine. Now she gets her spiritual nourishment directly from the level that is above the two of them, which is called the "Big Mother." She grows up until she is equal—even a little bit higher because she is called "The Crown" and the crown is above the head—and then they find interest in each other. So they come back, face to face, and this means they are equal, only different voices. They are not the same. Each one of them is a different energy, beyond cycles or linear concepts. We have different names for it in the Kabbalah. They have become different but equal. However, she can go higher than him and give him something that he doesn't have because she is connected to Big Mother. She is a part of the Big Mother. All of this was written in codes in the sixteenth century, and it is a prophecy. I see that we are exactly in the stage of turning face to face. Now it is obvious that women are equal. We have the concept of equal rights for women even within the old structure of a patriarchal and chauvinist society. Now we come face to face. And woman, she will be above, with the Big Mother over us all.

The Big Mother

A Spiritual Renewal   To Blend   With the Source
A Wisdom   From the Holiest
Of Holy   A Deep   And Sacred
Place Of Mysticism

Outside the Borders   Connect   With Infinity
A Giving Space   Nurtured
By the Gaia Tradition

The Big Mother   The Crown of Woman
In Unity   With Man   In Love
And Devotion   Coming Together
A Study Group   The Place   And the Space Open
To All

Protect   The Cycles   Of an Emerging   World
Regenerate   Creation
The Birth   Of   New Worlds

The sacred Aboriginal colors of Earth are red, yellow, black, and white. Red is the blood and the energy of fire. Black is the earth and the circle fires left by the Spirit Ancestors. Yellow is the water and the body of the Rainbow Serpent. White is the star, the air, and the sky Spirit Ancestors who came to Earth. In Dreamtime, the creation mystery is guided by ancestral beings from the Pleiades, the Seven Sisters. We are the custodians of the planet, caretakers for a living entity. *Blood of their blood, bone of their bone.*

Out of creativity comes the perpetuation of a cosmic union, a bridge that connects the world of the sacred with the world of the profane. It is a creative retreat of space and color and sound that merges without words into a communion of all beings and ancient stories.

3

Breaking the Stone

Healing the Waters

DESIREE FITZGIBBON
Tasmanian Celtic Shaman

"It was in Lalai—
The Beginning, the Dreamtime—
That the Wandjina
Appeared from the sky,
With their heads
Surrounded by circles
Of lightning,
And thunder,
And dressed in a curtain
Of rain."

MUDROOROO, AUSTRALIAN ABORIGINAL
AUTHOR OF *Aboriginal Mythology*

DESIREE FITZGIBBON

Raised in Tasmania, Desiree is a descendant of Celtic lineage. She is a gifted speaker and has received permission from the Aboriginal women Elders to share these teachings. A true artist in the very essence of the word, her works are exhibited internationally and in private collections in Tasmania, Canada, and the United States. Desiree's canvases are a synthesis of experience, a search for language to express the intrinsic patterning of the land and the patterns held in the memory of space. As a mother and teacher, she is currently spearheading the development of Temenus, a creative and spiritual retreat center for international artists situated in light forest on a secluded bay in Dunalley, Tasmania.

The Pleiades, also known as the Seven Sisters, are the strong and guiding star group of the Aboriginal people. My connections to a particular woman in western Australia are what led me to the Aboriginal carriers of the wisdom from the Seven Sisters. There are a lot of stories about the Pleiades, about how they were beings who came through the stars to this star. Even today, the people are still guided by the Pleiades.

During the early 1990s I attended a workshop at a monastery in New South Wales. It was taught by an Aboriginal woman, an Elder. She had intentionally drawn together a group of white Australian women who were in the healing professions, and she shared with us a lot of stories. We shared together the secret healing wisdoms, the rites of passage and the rituals. These involve the use of medicine stones, herbs, bush flowers, and remedies that are indigenous to Australia. The rituals pertaining to Dreamtime Law are called "business," and there is law called "women's business." At our gathering we were taught some women's business which I am not at liberty to share. However, some of the teachings were for cleansing and the healing of illness. The Aborigines use eucalyptus. In the community, they actually smoke out entire houses with it for clearing. The eucalyptus is burned, similar to the Native American tradition of burning sage. We were pleased to hear that a hospital in New South Wales had accepted this tradition and acknowledged that this practice is an important thing to do. The hospital is using the Aboriginal method of healing in the emergency rooms. These rooms hold the spirits which pass through, and they need to be cleared and cleansed because the people who come through them are not in a well state. The workshop was not a long time for us to be together. However, there were a lot of teachings.

The Aborigines use stones in a lot of their rituals. There was a particular ritual that we were given from the story called "The Breaking of the Stone." As the story goes, a particular group of Elders were in the desert keeping sacred stones and waiting for a time when the Star People would direct them to break these stones in ritual. At the appropriate time, the Aborigines called together all the teachers and Elders of their race. Together they drew a symbolic map of the sacred sites in Australia where the stones were to be broken. This ritual had to begin in the summertime. When I heard about the ritual, it had been happening for a few years. The final stone was broken in 1995, sometime between February and May. When the final stone was broken, it signified the time of the Dreaming Tracks. The Dreaming Tracks are energy lines that go around the Earth. Upon completion of the ritual, the Dreaming Tracks were fully opened. It is said that with the breaking of the final stone, we have ten years to get things right on this planet. After ten years, the Dreaming Tracks will be closed and it will be too late. That is in the year 2005. The Dreaming Tracks are different from the traditional song line maps of the Spirit Ancestors' journeys, which represent the creative journeys of the Star Ancestors and the sacred sites where they arose.

This was the sort of story we shared and we were told to go out and share the stories with the world. Now is the time for them to be given. I had been very much drawn to Utopia, a women's place in the central desert of Australia. At Utopia women are creating art on silk using a Batik method. This art was a major beginning of the movement of Aboriginal Women's Art—sacred art which is coming out and being exhibited for the first time in various art centers all over the world. This movement certainly benefited the community. The Aborigines' experience of the white man coming to their land has paralleled that of indigenous peoples in other parts of the world. Alcohol is a big problem in their community, and they have seen the loss of their cultural stories and the loss of their honor. Through the creation of art, people can actually share their stories and once again achieve recognition for their wisdom.

Traditionally, Aboriginal women hold the wisdom. You will find this as well in the Irish and Scottish way, where the Celtic Grandmothers are the keepers of the wisdom. The keepers of the wisdom are the women and they are coming into their power now.

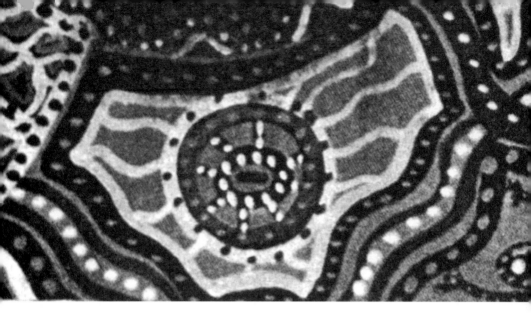

ABORIGINAL ABSTRACT
by Jingalu

Several of the Aboriginal women are producing art that transcends any label. The imagery is globally accepted. It is not necessarily traditional dot painting; some of the art is likened to abstract expressionism. To me, it is an offering of expression that is guided by ancestral beings, a vehicle that connects to the original stories. They are coded texts from all dimensions. The paintings hold codices that we recognize in our own psyche, that we have knowledge of in our DNA.

We, the Celts and the Druids, have our own codices and texts, such as the stone circles and the symbolic spiral. The spiral symbol connected me to the legends of my Celtic ancestors; like ancient runes, spiral stone relics write to us on common ground. Tasmania, my homeland, was founded as a convict settlement. The first white people who came here were either military personnel or convicts who had been sentenced to exile for stealing a loaf of bread, or a horse, or whatever. My dispossessed ancestors walked the land here—on these sands. But those of us who live here now were never really given a sense of pride about our ancestry. There was more a sense of shame—if you came from convict stock—and we would never have thought to look back and find out where our people came from. I did not give enough weight to the Druidic knowledge that was part of my lineage. I was searching for a place for myself in culture and in history.

I was first introduced to the spiral through my study of the Hopi culture, and then I started seeking it out in other cultures. Where does this spiral appear? Why is it that we relate to it so much? I also found the spiral to be very strong in Ireland. There is one Irish symbol with three interlinking spirals that represent woman's sacred place. I continued to research about the Irish, the Scots, and the French. I studied the Cianic stones of France. These are hundreds and hundreds of stones set in two long rows. The Cianic stones are also one of the major European sites of standing stone circles. Here my fascination for the language of stones began. That led into research concerning spirals on stones, such as the Celtic knot.

Five years ago I went to a conference in Scotland and had a major awakening. I found my roots there, and I am really proud of my heritage. In a way, I suppose, I had been carrying that badge of shame endemic to thinking white people who know what has happened to indigenous people around the world. It is not something that we always want to talk about, even though the tribes of Europe have suffered their own massacres. It comes back to that—in the end it is all about the blood that we share. We have all been through massacres. We are all responsible for them, and we have all been victims of them in our consciousness. I'm moving to a place now where I am just open to the ancient ancestral Teachings. If I can share them in a respectful way and with gratitude for what I have been given, then I feel that it is okay to be white.

When I talk about the Teachings, I use the word "Ancestors," and I use that in a very broad sense. If I am with the stones and I live with the stones they are my "allies." I receive teachings through the stones and often hold them in my hands at night when I am seeking clarity. They seem to draw me to certain places. I get sensations and imagery, often relating to events that happened in the place where I am at the time. I call the stones my ancestors, too, as I do the trees. I always honor a tree as my ancestor. In every journey that I am drawn on, I am given another fragment of the tablet. I come home with another fragment and I have to find a place for it to fit with everything else that has been given to me.

In Australia there are many places where uranium mining is going on. In Kakadu, which is a wetlands, the mining is occurring as we speak. This area is probably one of the most pristine wetlands environments left on the planet. Kakadu is home to a huge variety of bird populations, and it is also where the Mirra people live in their traditional way. They are now coming forward to speak out against the uranium because there are leaks and it is causing great harm to their environment. It is not as safe as the authorities are reporting.

Around all of this, pertaining to the water, are the Rainbow Serpent Teachings. The keeper of the waters is the Rainbow Serpent, as similar to the symbols of other cultures: in Maya we have the Feathered Serpent, Quetzalcoatl and Ku-Kul-Can; Lord Krishna is linked with a half-bird, half-man and the serpent of infinity; Adam and Eve and the serpent; in Buddhism, the serpent ascended humanity into Nirvana. There have been a lot of celebrations and initiations to open up the way for the Rainbow Serpent in these days.

I received another teaching from an Aboriginal woman Elder who lived on Flinders Island, which is near where I live. Flinders Island is the "Island of the Moon Bird," and a sacred place on the song line. There is also a very strong community there and on other nearby islands. What the Elder told me was that the way we are to heal this planet is through creativity; the teaching of the Rainbow Serpent is creativity.

I created a painting called "Healing the Waters." While I was working on the painting, I felt as though I was actually working with the blood—the blood of the people and the blood of Earth, which is the waters. If the contaminated toxins are allowed into the underground water systems, then we are in very big trouble. As soon as there is a drought and we have to tap into the subterranean water supply, it becomes a huge problem—really huge. So the Mirra people—who are the keepers of the land where the uranium is being mined, Kakadu—are fighting a strong battle at this time against the multinational mining companies and the Australian government, which granted leases to those companies. There are other places in the western desert where they are mining and keeping very quiet about their activities. People know, however. We export most of the uranium from Australia, but we still have to deal with the waste.

I haven't even touched the surface of what Australia has to offer. It is a very old, pristine country—a very wise country. I think that if we would listen to the way of the Kakadu Elders, about caring for our country, we would send out a global message: *We must work toward keeping our rivers clean and protecting our sacred waters.*

I feel as though I hardly know anything, but I've been given some information—from the Elders, the wisdom keepers, and the stones. I'm trying to be perceptive about what's around me. Lately, I've been discovering markings on the beach where I live. Snails, creatures from the sea, are making hieroglyphics in the sand. I feel as though they are encoding me, waking up my knowledge.

I have been given permission by the Aboriginal Grandmothers to speak. I have been careful about how much I can share, even through the paintings. I'm keeping a boundary around that knowledge. I see myself sitting on the ground around water holes, working with the natural ochers of Earth: the natural pigments, the raw umbers and the clay colors. I have a strong sense that we are being called to celebrate, to dance, to sing—to pass the stones on in that way. I don't want to stand in front of bulldozers anymore. If I'm killed, I'm no use to anyone. I want to be celebrating what we have and passing that information on to the young people. Then they can remember the stories and they can begin to care for their land, care for their Earth. So, my paintings are healings, stepping-stones, vehicles for expressing what I know; vehicles to travel through and gain more information within deep meditation.

STANDING STONES

Seven years ago I visited the Hopi Elders. I brought with me important stones as talking allies. It was during that visit that I began a series of paintings. I've continued to work on that series during subsequent visits. Last year a painting came, as part of that series. The painting is on pink-red ochre Earth, and it is two ghostly figures who are joined in the heart. They are dancing free, joined in the heart, like the sacred twins of Hopi mythology.

I have been painting on large canvas—eight to ten feet—for the past twelve years. I feel the need to say something big, and so I roll out a canvas on the floor and wash it with paint and a broom. Years ago, in school, the head of the art department told me that I was audacious for painting so big. My response was to ask why and remind him that men have been painting on large canvas forever. I met a woman in the desert who also painted like this, and I felt she gave me permission to keep doing this. So I continue to paint big. My feeling is that it won't be just me sitting on Earth painting to heal the waters. Tibetan monks with their sand paintings, Native

Americans with their drums, Aborigines with their didgeridoos—people from all cultures will come together to share their paintings, their songs, and their music, like a caravan of people moving around Earth, healing the waters.

I entreat people to listen to the stones. The stones are singing. They are all awake, and they are all vibrant with information. Go and sit with them—wherever you are—and ask, and they will share with you whatever you are ready to learn. Honor them in their own place—for so often they are turned into things on the marketplace like sapphires on women's necklaces and it's not the same thing. These stones, they know it all. They have been here before us.

The Breaking of the Stones, the stony people. The Star People guided the Teachings about the stones. The Aboriginal keepers were waiting for the moment when the Star People said this had to begin, and they acted as soon as they received that information, whether through dreams, prophecy, song, trance, or meditation. Whichever way the message came, the people acted as the Star People instructed.

The Star People, the Star Friends, the Guardians, the Dear Ones, the Helpers—I don't think it matters what we call them. Our awareness of them needs to be sharpened. They are here for us, and if we need them we can call on them at any time. We can look up to the stars as a reminder that they are out there for us. I have no color or shape or style to explain what I am talking about. I just know that the voices are there, and I know that I am to listen to the voices.

Healing the Waters

Rainbow Serpent Woman   Sister   From the Sky

Spirit Ancestors   Defining

All Space   All Time   In a Nameless World

Of Great Power   Healing   The Waters

Voices   A Dreamtime   A Songline

A Teaching   The Law   Residing

At the Birthing Place   A Spiritual Power

Activated Through Ritual   At Sacred Sites

Healing the Waters

Dream Tracks   Open   The Breaking of the Stone

A Feminine Principle   Divine Fertility

First Women   On Earth   The Seven Sisters

The Pleiades   Healing   The Waters

Blood   Of Their Blood

Bone   Of Their Bone

A Cosmic Union   Of All Beings

And   All Ancient   Stories

The spiritual Fire of Unity has been kindled on behalf of our Mother Earth and ALL of her inhabitants. As we live in this time of the fifth world, all the four sacred powers are being reunited. They are the colors of Humankind—the Redman, Whiteman, Yellowman, and Blackman. In this time of healing, rituals that have been forgotten will be brought back: art, music, song, dance, spiritual wisdom and knowledge. The wisdom of how to work with Mother Earth will be restored. Female energy will heal the planet—nurturing, loving, touching, and sharing. In preparation for the Reunion day of the Eagle of the North, and the Condor of the South (Americas) we pray together again. The spinal column of the Earth is in South America. The energy pattern of the grid lines is the feminine—the Motherland. The memory of the woman and the birth of the New Earth come through the memory of the Motherland. Only through the solar initiation can the sleeping body of mankind be awakened, in unity, in prayer. Through this illumination the true sons and daughters of the new teachings will travel as lightning to pierce through the shadows that envelop the human race and prepare to receive the memories of the luminosity.

4

Tribal Ink and Link

Awakening Humanity

LUIS E. MEJIA
Colombian Muisica Journalist

*The Golden Sun Disc of Lemuria was not made
of ordinary gold, but was transmuted gold, and
unusual in its qualities in that it was a translucent metal similar, evidently, to the metal of the
UFOs you can almost look through.*

BROTHER PHILIP, MONASTERY
OF THE SEVEN RAYS ANDES, PERU

LUIS E. MEJIA

Luis E. Mejia was born in Bogota, Colombia. He is a Muisica Indian, a descendant of the inhabitants of South America. He was initiated by the Kogi of the Sierra Nevada mountains in Colombia and the Quero in Cuzco, Peru. Luis is a journalist and creator of Tribal Ink Inc., the Native America and Eco-News Network, which captures the heartbeat of the indigenous communities of North, South, and Central America.

Luis is the only person I have ever met who knows how to create a light frequency within crystals, which he uses for healing people and the planet.

Thank you for giving me this opportunity to share with the world! The beautiful beginning of my life was in Bogota, Colombia. Ever since my childhood I have had a deep love for seeking truth in the mystery of spirit. At the age of four, I had my first near-death experience—with water. I was chasing a ball, and after falling I went under water, remaining submerged for several minutes. Luckily someone saved me. Deep down inside, however, the guardian spirits have remained in contact with me.

I have an uncle who is a Franciscan priest. He taught me, from a very early age, a deep reverence and love for nature and animals. His brother, my father, was a surgeon. To my disappointment, my father moved our family to the United States, where he could further his career. Growing up, I was always the black sheep of the family because I frequently had psychic experiences. At night, while lying on my bed, there would be a complete force field around me—covering me. I often saw spacecraft in Dreamtime. These experiences eventually led me into the study of the occult.

Years later, in 1986, I had another near-death experience. I was in an almost fatal car crash. After hitting a tree, head on, while traveling at a very high speed, I narrowly escaped death. When that happened, the spirit guardians told me that I had better change my lifestyle or I would not be around much longer. This experience eventually led me to return home to Colombia on a spiritual search for a more truthful life path. I also began reading more about UFOs.

My academic field of interest was journalism and communications. In South America I met members of MUFON (Mutual UFO Network) and we became friends. Through these new acquaintances I went on my first UFO investigation. We were investigating an occurrence outside Bogota in a small town called Tenjo, where a "campesino," an uneducated farmer, had been picked up by a spacecraft and dropped off eighteen hours later. He ended up in a town almost 300 miles away—totally disoriented. I went to meet him. He took me to a sacred site called "Bosque de Nuesa," Forest of Nuts.

This is an incredible area with a beautiful lake and llamas running wild. There were huge mushrooms growing. This was a very mystical area with a lot of Deva spirits. A Deva kingdom, in fact. He took me there to make contact with spacecraft. We did!

I returned to the United States to continue my spiritual quest. I began my studies with the Brahma Kumaris. This is a world spiritual University of Raja Yoga Meditation. This is an open-eyed meditation using thought for self-mastery and well-being. Raja means sovereign, and Yoga means union. Through pure thought you can connect with a source—a higher power, a being of light. In Raja Yoga you learn to focus internally to find a place of serenity. This is a place of empowerment from a source of light, an endless source of light. All of this you do with your eyes open! The University was founded in 1937 through Prajapita Brahma, who had a series of visions revealing the inevitable destruction and re-evolution of civilization through direct intervention by Higher Powers. The teachings return humanity to the root values of humankind and the

CHICHÉN ITZÁ

equality of the sexes in all aspects of life. The university is located on Mount Abu in Rajasthan, India. It is a refuge for the free exchange of thoughts and ideas to embody the teachings of global harmony for humanity and the environment.

When I first journeyed to India I had a very powerful experience in the Himalayas which connected me to the ancient system of Ayurvedic Medicine—a healing practice. Since my father was a doctor I was familiar with Western medicine—the illnesses and cures—and I easily developed an interest in nontraditional medicine. I went to Nepal for further studies and it was there that I began to photograph ventricular clouds. These are clouds that are shaped like spacecraft. In fact, the craft hide themselves in those cloud formations. Thus I began to document my journey.

In 1995, my entire UFO experience and initiation with indigenous Elders began. I traveled to the Yucatan to meet with Hunbatz Men, the Mayan Elder who is a keeper and interpreter of the Mayan calendar. I participated in the March 21st spring equinox solar initiation. The Mayan word for extraterrestrial is "Moxul." I was at the sacred site of Chichén Itzá, which means "People of the Well."

Chichén Itzá is also called the City of the Serpent Kulkulcan, the Great Father. After the ceremony I wanted to remove myself from the crowd for solitude and inner reflection. I walked to the Ball Court where there is a vacuum of energy, which literally allows one to hear cosmic sound. I sat near two round columns. I began to meditate using chants and Tibetan bells for toning. Toning is a vocal practice using voice as an instrument for mantras. On my right, the sun was casting an extraordinary light which was coming between these pillars to me. As a result of the March equinox light as well as the sacred site, I became activated. I could recall the past knowledge and wisdom of the Maya and the purpose of the astronomical alignments.

There, in Chichén Itzá, I met a man named Don Barbaachano, who is the patriarch of la Familia Barbaachano. I would not have been able to visit Chichén Itzá if it had not been for Don Barbaachano, who was raised by a Shaman. His family was largely responsible for opening up the pyramidal sites for public education purposes. He shared a deeper knowledge of the Mayan site with me.

In the Yucatan, I met another powerful shaman from Venezuela whose name is Domingo Dios Puerta. Domingo is Sunday. Dios is God. Puerta is door. His teachings are about the maize, the sacred corn. He is also connected to what is occurring in Bolivia at Lake Titicaca where there is a subterranean city.

This city is where the true White Brotherhood resides—the Brotherhood of the Seven Rays which they call the Illuminated Ones. At Lake Titicaca, there exists an underground city, a fifth-dimensional city where the Golden Disc of Muru is. Before the Incas, Lord Muru of Lemuria came to Lake Titicaca with sacred scrolls and the Golden Disc. There is a book called *The Secret of the Andes* by Brother Philip, which contains the encoded memory of lost worlds and the coming of the Space Masters. Near Lake Titicaca reside the monoliths of Tiahuanaco, which were built by a pre-Incan civilization. Tiahuanaco was once a coastal port of Lemuria, part of the lost Pacific coast of Mu. During the destruction of Mu, Tiahuanaco rose

VENTRICULAR CLOUDS

out of the sea and Lake Titicaca was formed. This was the last pole shift on this planet, which caused the upheaval. Later on, the Incas traveled in search of the Golden Disc and built ceremonial centers on top of the ruins of Lemuria. These ruins were made initially from huge stones cut by light energy. This light technology was used to transport objects and human beings. The Incan Priests hid the Golden Disc where it remains today. I became like a feather in the wind being introduced to all the amazing sacred sites and teachers of ancient knowledge. Each teacher was giving me a piece of the puzzle, and I in turn would give other people pieces of the puzzle.

In 1997, my life took another turn. I ended up working in corporate America for Ford Motor Company. I was sent to Brazil for a year. This was the beginning of my introduction to the energy of the Amazon and the Indian peoples of that region. There are people in Brazil awaiting the return of the extraterrestrials. Brazil is built in a unique geographical area; it is part of the heart of South America. Outside Sao Paulo, about three hours away, there is a mystical triangle. This triangle consists of three towns—Trés Corações,

LAKE TITICACA

Varginha, and São Tomes de las Letras. At one time the earth moved and lifted the third town—São Tomes de las Letras—into a plateau. There are amazing slab stone rock formations, underneath which is a UFO base. There are extraordinary numbers of petroglyphs surrounded by waterfalls. People within this mystical triangle of three towns are in contact with spacecraft. The ships appear and it is considered very commonplace to see them clearly.

I discovered that Brazil is covered with crystals. The extraterrestrials receive electromagnetic energy from the crystals. All of the crystals I have are from Brazil. I dug them up from the earth myself. This is where I first encountered the crystal skull. These skulls are cut against the grain, even though modern science tells us that if you cut any crystal against the grain, it shatters. The crystal skull is an ancient computer brought back to man's consciousness now. The DNA strains are reconnecting at this time. That is why we now see the Indigo children, the Blue Ray babies—children who are coming in with a whole different DNA pattern. The crystal skulls are coming back into the consciousness of humankind because they have been through the cycles and are encoded with the memories of our past. The skull activates your center—totally activates your center. It is very important for people who carry the teachings to have balance within their mind-body-spirit dimension. The teachings hold the knowledge of Tibet, Egypt, India, Maya, Hopi. So, one's inner center must be not only activated but in balance.

The energy of South America is the feminine energy. She is the Motherland. The memory of the woman is in the Amazon. At this time Earth is being reborn through the feminine energy. A 6,000-pound skull came from the Atacama desert in Chile at the Valley of the Moon. This is where NASA goes to test their moon launch. The whole area looks exactly like the moon. This is where the Earth Keepers are. The Earth Keepers are the crystals. Near La Serena, in Chile, I had another major UFO experience. The whole area looks like Tibet. I connected with a woman named La Hermana Gladys, Sister Gladys. She has been involved with the UFO phenomenon for twenty years. In the place where she lives the whole valley lights up.

She performs the *Agniharta,* the fire ceremony. This is a fire meditation, which is done with a copper pyramid placed upside down. This ceremony is done at the exact hour of sunrise and the exact hour of sunset using cow dung and purified butter, which is burned and—together with the pyramid—creates a resonance field. This ritual is enhanced by particular songs. The ashes from the fire heal people. The ashes also make plants grow incredibly large and take fungus and disease out of them. You can eat the ashes by putting them in your food, which is a very curative medicine.

In Córdoba, Argentina, there is another fifth dimensional city. There are faces carved into the stones covering this city. I met a woman there named Beatrice Citzo. She writes Egyptian hieroglyphics backwards. I have met her and I also have read her writings. From the time that she was a little girl she experienced leaving her body. She would literally float out of the window. Beatrice is connected to the Andes Illuminated Brotherhood, who are guarding and protecting the Andes. They are holding and disseminating the ancient teachings.

When I was sent to South America in 1997 to do my corporate work I began to have all these activations. By that I mean the awakening of mind-body-spirit. I began moving in and out of other dimensions where I have lived before. In South America there is a grid pattern of energy waves, which forms a pyramid. The equator runs right through southern Colombia. When you are on the equator you are vibrating at a completely different frequency. The line of the equator separates the North and South energy of Gaia—Mother Earth.

The Kogi, in the Sierra Nevada of Colombia, are living in the teachings called *Aluna.* They are maintaining the heartbeat of Mother Earth. At this time we are living in 3-D—the third dimension of the time/space continuum. We are vibrating at a higher frequency than before because we are passing through the Photon Belt. Earth also is vibrating at a higher level. There are certain places where the land is like a heart chakra. These certain places are the acupressure points of Earth's meridians. Earth also needs activation with the crystals to anchor energy and balance the meridian pathways. When you travel to certain sacred sites like Machu Picchu, Tikal, and Lake Titicaca and you perform ceremonies with intent, you are reactivating your past history—the times when you were an initiate of the ancient orders. In fact, you are stepping out of time and becoming a time traveler. This is what the Maya teach. For instance, by being together in Costa Rica at the June 21, 1999, Solstice ceremony, we reactivated the site of Itzaru. All of us who gathered there from North, South, and Central America also reactivated our memories, our genetic codes. Again, the condor of the South and the eagle of the North are uniting the Ancient People's wisdom.

I returned to South America during the winter of 1999. I always say I was taken out of the Andes without my permission because I was carried out as a young child by my parents. However, I always knew I would return to serve my people. That is why I have the condor feather—to carry me back home safely.

My whole purpose is to be a bridge: the tribal ink and the link—the media bridge. This is what I do. The teachings have been passed on secretly for thousands of years to select people who have

Secret of the Andes

been the guardians. And now the teachings are being released. As the time comes for the change of cycles, we begin to realize we are part of the "One Hand." The knowledge is presently being reactivated. A beam of light encoded with information will awaken your memories. That is why your dreams are so important. In Dreamtime, you step out of time.

Look at the cycles of time. You have a Golden Age, a Silver Age, a Copper Age, and an Iron Age. Then you have the Confluence Age. We are at the end of a cycle, and between cycles is called the Confluence. Next we enter the Diamond Age. At this current time all the knowledge is being released. When you ask yourself "who am I?" the answer is one of those divine beings from Atlantis or Lemuria. What are those times? They are but the memory of the Golden Age, when we remember a Paradise on Earth. There will come a time when you will be in the right place at the right time.

When I work with Earth crystals I create a light frequency inside of the crystal. By rubbing the two charged crystals together, balls of light are activated. When you know how to work with the crystals you create a neuro-linguistic program. In all the sacred sites I activate the light frequency within the crystals and then break them to feed Earth. I also give a piece of crystal to each person at the ceremonial site. Then we are connected to that place in Earth, as an anchor of light. Crystals are transformers of light. I'm giving this crystal to you, which I brought from Brazil. [At this time, Luis gives me a beautiful standing crystal with a pyramidal formation at the top.]

While I stayed in Colombia, I met some people who had just come back from the Sierra Nevada de San Marta. They told me about the energy shift that was occurring there as a result of the revolutionaries and the increasing jungle warfare. I began having dreams about the Kogi. I wanted to visit the Kogi, but sudden plans took me stateside. I began searching for a book by Alan Herrera called *In the Heart of the World*. Instead, I found another book called *Elder Brother Speaks*. I bought this book. Since I am a journalist I also always collect articles. Well, I was going through some magazines, and three of them fell off the shelf! One was *Kindred*

Spirit from 1989, and the cover story was about the Kogi. I asked myself: What is this? So I began reading the book *Elder Brother Speaks* about the Kogi. In fact, I couldn't put it down until, that is, I fell deeply asleep. The next thing I knew I was out of my body—like astral projection—all the way to the Sierra Nevada. I was there. It was as if the Kogi pulled me. I remember very clearly leaving my body like I was doing a somersault and then landing in this beautiful mountain range with the Kogi. This kind of experience had not occurred since my childhood. It was very surprising. I was not asking for the experience, so I was not prepared. I just fell asleep after having read the book. After that I quit my job with Ford Motor Company and a week later I was in Colombia at this conference—the second gathering of Priests and Elders of the Americas—when the Kogi appeared.

Soon I became a translator for the Kogi, to help build a bridge between the North and South Americas—the eagle and the condor. We went into the Amazon jungle and put up a teepee for a peyote ceremony. Some of the Kogi stayed with us to participate in the circle. We sang and shared our cultures. I continued to translate the English of the Navajo and the Dine' into the Kogi language and Spanish. The link was incredible! I ended up returning with the Kogi up into the lands of the Sierra Nevada mountains. I spent two weeks there—going through initiation with prayer and fasting. I also went through a confession ceremony. The Kogi read my mind. This was a most beautiful experience for me, and I remained there with the Kogi elders, the Mamas, and the whole community. They taught me their teachings of Aluna. Since that time I have returned twice. The Kogi are living in the consciousness of Aluna. Their teachings of the law of origin are held with the Mamas in the heart of the world. I learned there are two more lost cities in that mountain range. There is also a stone map, which is eight feet tall. This stone has encoded geometric patterns on the surface. This stone appears in the BBC film *In the Heart of the World*. I've not yet been to the Lost City of the Andes. It is a three-day walk into the jungle or you can go part-way by helicopter. I will make that journey someday soon. The Kogi have been bringing me back to the Sierra Nevada in Dreamtime. Soon I will see them again. For now, I urge you to visit South America, to go to the ancient sites. I will continue to perform ceremonies with the crystals to rejuvenate the places of our past, to awaken the *Apu*, which is the Quechua word for "Spirits of the Mountains." Our work in South America is to balance the wreckage of industry which is digging and disrupting Mother Earth. The mountains have fallen out of balance, and Earth is in shock.

By performing ceremony with intent, an energetic pattern is created which will restore the balance. Quantum physics describes all phenomena as wave patterns. In your mind your consciousness is like a beam of light. Simply speaking, when you send a laser beam of light in wave patterns into an interference pattern you can create a hologram—a third-dimensional image. Then you could travel faster than the speed of light throughout the universe, and you would end up back where you began. When you travel faster than the speed of light, you are bending time and space. Time starts to slow down, and this is when a time warp occurs. When you work with the crystals with intent and you know how to create a light frequency a hologram results. This becomes a vehicle. What creates peace in music? The space between the notes. What creates peace of mind? The space between thoughts. In your own mind you

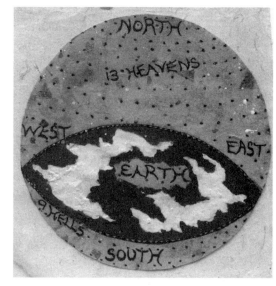

DRAWINGS OF THE MAYAN
THIRTEEN HEAVENS
AND NINE HELLS
by Tula

can manifest a wave pattern to restore balance. Our human process of observation affects the outcome of where energy goes. When you consciously go to a sacred site and use healing with vocal singing or toning, you are using sound as an energy pattern. This pattern interacts with light, interacts with matter, which raises your vibration. This ascension brings you into another dimension—a fourth dimension, a fifth dimension. You can actually step into the middle of your soul's life. Then the activation of past lives is possible. This is activation. All past lives are recorded on pinnacles of light. The coccyx bone is the first bone created in the embryo. This is the temple of your codes. The whole spinal column is connected to the whole spine of Earth. What connects the North and South? North America and South America are connected by the North and South magnetic poles. The Indian people are traveling back and forth to perform ceremonies in order to restore the balance. This is why the Kogi opened up the heart of the world.

The Star Ancestors are now re-awakening certain people who are the remnant cultures of Lemuria and Atlantis. When Atlantis fell, the Priests and Priestesses knew what was coming, and they instructed people to migrate with the sacred teachings. Part of the reason Atlantis fell was because of the misuse of crystal firestone energy. The crystal firestone light kept with the Golden Disc was used to move objects and people through space. The stone was red and shaped like a diamond. Now the extraterrestrials are here and helping us to ascend. They are continuing to observe us as we move toward the year 2004. At this moment, there is a grand plan for this planet as we travel through time and space. In South America we have Machu Picchu, Lake Titicaca, Nazca lines, Tiahuanaco . . . many temples of understanding. Now is the time for sharing. South America is the spinal column of Mother Earth's body. We are the backbone of the Earth. Our sacred sites are the meridians connecting the chakras. The crown chakra, the third eye, the throat, the heart, are Earth's doorways to knowledge. Follow the grid patterns, the beacons, for now is the time for wisdom to come forth.

Awakening Humanity

Crystal Beams   Of Wave Patterns   A Neuro-Linguistic
Language of Light   Frequency Transformers   Feeding
The Earth   Anchors   For Sacred Sites   Beacons
For Sky Walkers   Bones   Of Crystalline Energy
To Heal   Mother Earth

Crystal Skulls   Encoded Memories   Return
To Humanity   Consciousness   Connect
The Strains   The DNA   Descendents
Of Ancient Times   Activate   Your Center
Balance   Body-Mind-Spirit
Enter   The Fifth Dimension   Beyond Time
Space   Matter   Energy

Follow   The Rays   Inside
A Subterranean Temple   The Golden Disc
Translucent   An Object of Transportation
Raised   Into Etheric Realms   Of Our Cosmic Sun
Opening   The Crown Chakras   Of Our Illumination

A classified document from the Director of Special Projects for the Alien Contact Intelligence Organization (ACIO) to all members of the Labyrinth group—a secret cosmic group of humans and aliens) indicates that the Wingmakers—a civilization of advanced consciousness that comprehends the universal systems that govern existence, or at least the laws of time and space—strategically placed seven time capsules on this planet including the one found at the Ancient Arrow site at Choco Canyon in New Mexico. The first of these was an optical disk containing twenty-three segments in the form of petroglyphs and hieroglyphic symbols. According to the ACIO, the artifacts embedded within this optical disk found in chambers below Earth's surface represent well over eight thousand pages of text that predict the future of the human race approximately 750 years from now.

5

Truth

The Brotherhood of the Snake

AGENT DANIEL M. SALTER
French Comanche Former CIA/NRO Agent

> *"Do not let the military and the industrial weapons builders control all the power."*
>
> PRESIDENT EISENHOWER

AGENT DANIEL M. SALTER

Agent Daniel M. Salter is a retired counter-intelligence agent for the Scientific and Technical Unit of Interplanetary Phenomena. He was a CONRAD courier for President Eisenhower and a member of the Pilot Air Force, the National Reconnaissance Office (NRO), the CIA, and the Development of Conscious Contact Citizenry Department (DCCCD), with the United States military. He taught courses on electromagnetic anti-gravitational propulsion systems as a professor emeritus at Mountain View College in Texas. Of Comanche and French descent, Daniel is the father of three and grandfather of three. A man with a mission, he has a brilliant mind and one of the most extensive film and reading library on the history of UFOs that I have ever encountered.

We have already made contact with civilizations on four other planets within our universe. In the military we teach our Air Force officers, as they go through the ranks, that this contact has already been made. This knowledge has been carried for more than fifty years, since 1947. The military has a responsibility to tell people about our contact with these civilizations. If we don't, we bypass the whole Constitution of the United States. The real problem that inhibits the release of this knowledge lies within the fossil fuel-based energy industry. The extraterrestrials offer technology through which we could have free energy. We have the potential to use the energy around the smallest molecule to that around the largest universe. It is this electromagnetic propulsion system which will make our current energy industry obsolete. This is the greatest danger that the government sees—the transition from big-money fossil fuel companies to free energy for everyone. Under the Eisenhower administration, the federal government decided to bypass the constitution and form a treaty with extraterrestrials. The treaty was called 1954 Greada Treaty. This treaty is documented in the Disclosure Project in Washington, D.C., and is further described in Steven M. Greer's book *Disclosure* which includes the testimony of Agent Don Phillips who witnessed a film of the Eisenhower/ET meeting at an undisclosed location. The aliens, however, are going to force the hand of destiny. If we [the United States Government] don't tell the general population about extraterrestrial contact and the propulsion system, they will. When they have made contact with enough people, they will reveal that contact has been made between the U.S. government and extraterrestrials. In Star Wars, which is known within the military as the Spaceship Defense Initiative, what was the prime directive given by the extraterrestrials? It was: You will not interfere with an emerging extraterrestrial population and you will stop exploding nuclear weapons. To understand this directive, you have to go back and look in the Star Wars records of the past fifty years. The research can be done. The facts are now available to the public.

The secrets of Los Alamos that scientist Wen Ho Lee is accused of giving to Formosa (Taiwan) are the secrets of electromagnetic propulsion and pulse beam laser weapons. We have been working on this technology since World War II. Now, if you'll remember, when Lee was under investigation by a Senate committee, one member of the committee, the senator in charge of the investigation, got up and addressed the entire Senate. He said that what Lee had given Formosa was the anti-gravitational electromagnetic propulsion system. This senator basically told the whole world that Lee had given the secrets to our pulse beam weapons. That's the reason the whole affair was silenced. After that, nobody was talking. If they did, someone would have to explain where that technology came from. Do you hear anybody talking about Lee, about what he actually

UFO

did? Do you hear the FBI trying to prosecute him? No. After all, Lee and his wife worked for the CIA and FBI, spying on communist China for us. If you followed the case and read the accounts surrounding the arrest of Lee, you will come to understand what I had personal knowledge of—as a result of my being in the Agency—long before the charges against Lee became public: Lee and his wife worked for the different secret intelligence agencies of the U.S. I know this truth.

We have been working on this technology since World War II when we first learned the Germans had already developed advanced "Zero Gravity" technology. I was in the Air Force for twenty-two years. I achieved a high level of security clearance—Top Secret Cosmos II. When I got out of the Air Force, the government approached me with an offer of work at another agency. I accepted and went to work for a new agency, the National Reconnaisance Office (NRO). At that time the Central Intelligence Agency (CIA), the National Reconnaissance Office (NRO), and the National Security Agency (NSA) were all housed in the same building complex in Virginia. All of the information we gathered from our first spy planes—the U-2, the A-12, and the Blackbird—went into that little complex. The NRO was a new organization. The President at that time was Eisenhower and he was a military man and he wanted somebody that he could blame if things went wrong: if secrets were exposed, or wars such as Korea and the increasingly risky conflict in Vietnam were not clearly won. He did not want to take the same point of view that the Defense Department and the Air Force had taken, which basically was the assumption that we could win any war at any risk, anywhere in the world. He wanted all departments under one agency to follow the Star Wars vision, and that is how the NRO came into being. The NRO was the umbrella agency that reported all of the activities going on in the building complex directly to Eisenhower. The activities happening at that time were, in fact, the Star Wars Intelligence Program.

The location of this building complex in Virginia is also where Maji (MJ-12, the UFO policy group) was formed after Roswell

HANNEBU

occurred in 1947. The CIA really grew out of Maji with its specific agenda to monitor the extraterrestrial problem. This whole history is documented by William Cooper, in his book *Behold a Pale Horse*. He was a good friend of mine. He did for the Navy what I did for the Air Force with regard to intelligence work.

The first government involved in the manufacturing of advanced systems of spacecraft technology was Germany. The first downed spacecraft ever found and recovered were in Brazil; one went down in 1931 and the other in 1932. The Germans bought them from the Brazilian government. Germany had a great spy ring, so naturally they heard about the spacecraft and struck a monetary deal with the Brazilian government. They transported the recovered craft to Germany on submarines. By 1935 the Germans had perfected the duplication of the extraterrestrial spacecraft, complete with anti-gravitational electromagnetic propulsion. The name for the craft was the RFC-1, and it was followed by the RFC-2, -3, and -4. Eventually it came to be known as the Hannebu.

There were two secret societies in Germany: the Thule Society and the Vril Society. These secret occult societies were actually established in pre-World War I Vienna. Their esoteric and occult ideas were born from ancient Sumerian texts and trance channelers or psychic mediums. The same underground secret doctrines had rejuvenated such orders as the Templars, the Neo-Templars, the Freemasons, the Rosicrucians, and the Illuminati—all prophesying

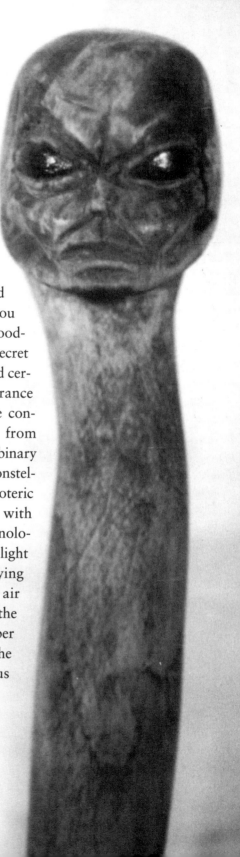

the impending arrival of the New Age. The Third Reich adopted these same ideas on occultism. Hitler named this New Age "The Black Sun" so that was what the Third Reich called it. This refers to the ending of the Piscean Era and the birth of the Aquarian Age. Hitler believed that he had been chosen to usher in the New Age, and his campaign of genocide was intended to purify the Aryan race in preparation for the New World Order. To be a member of the S.S., you had to be able to trace your Aryan bloodline back five generations. There were secret occult rituals performed as well as blood ceremonies. Through two particular trance mediums, the Thule Society had made contact with an advanced civilization from Aldebaran—a solar system based on binary suns that is located somewhere in the constellation we know as Orion. Both the esoteric studies and the communications with Aldebaran evolved into advanced technology such as the illuminated balls of light known as the Fou Fighters or Flying Tortoise—the unconventional Nazi air warfare weapon that displayed all the characteristics of a UFO. (In December 1944, Reuters published a report in the *New York Times* that a mysterious

EBE (EXTRATERRESTRIAL
BIOLOGICAL ENTITY)
by Stan Neptune

German warfare technology of a highly advanced nature was being used in the air against fighter bombers.) There is even speculation that the Third Reich attempted to create a time machine at the Messerschmitt factory in Germany.

Hitler believed that the Tibetans were descendants of the original strain of a more advanced race that had seeded Earth as the Gods of Babylonian Times. He sent his best genetic scientist to Tibet to study the people, that is, to measure the face, skull, feet—every aspect of the physical characteristics of their race.

By 1947 we knew that our powerful radar—one to five million megawatts of radiated energy—could interfere with the balance and navigation of extraterrestrial spacecraft. I had worked on a project to do that, to interfere with the navigation of extraterrestrial spacecraft. Where do we have most of our radar? White Sands, New Mexico. When the extraterrestrial spacecraft crashed near Roswell, we were already tracking them. There were actually two craft. One was completely destroyed. The other held three beings; one died in the crash and a second died soon after, but the third survived. That being lived in Los Alamos for three years. A botanist worked with him because, like a plant, he took energy from the sun. His system could not survive this environment. If you remember the sightings in the 1950s in Washington, D.C., that were reported several years after his capture—well, that was his command coming to retrieve him.

At that time I worked in a secret unit at Warner Robbins, Georgia. We were stationed at the Air Proving Ground Command at Eklund Air Force Base on temporary duty. This base is where the world's largest climatic hangar was; you could simulate being in the Antarctic or the desert, and this is where we ran tests using various simulated climates. But in Georgia I tested radar systems. We had a brilliant man named Thomas Townsend Brown who worked as an anti-gravity electromagnetic engineering scientist. We did not call the technology UFO; we called it an anti-gravitational propulsion system.

With the Philadelphia Experiment, we did not expect the ship *Etdinger* to disappear; it was only supposed to be made invisible to radar. Instead it physically disappeared and was transported two hundred miles to another harbor. We did not expect that. During the time of the Cold War, Russia had missiles. The U.S. government wanted to see the Russian bombers and missiles beyond the horizon. When you get to about two hundred and sixty miles in altitude radar can't follow the curvature of the earth. It shoots off the horizon and then we're unable to see their aircraft.) So we took about six acres in Alaska and put a powerful heat-generating radar over them which we aimed to a point up in the sky. What we created effectively was a heat-generating mirror. It was about three miles long and a mile wide. When this special radar beam is transmitted up, we can tilt the mirror and see over the horizon. When we erected this "Harp," a side effect was that we changed the weather. If you heat

PROPHECY ROCK AT ORABI *representing the Hopi prophecy that offers the choice between the technological Path of the Two-hearted that leads to the destruction, or the planting Path of the One-hearted, that leads to the Creator. Courtesy of the late David Monongye.*

up part of the ionosphere, that is going to change the weather. Now, we could also tilt the mirror and burn up part of the earth—Africa, Russia, anywhere around the globe—if we wanted to. All the vegetation would be gone. We could literally turn it into desert. We tried this two or three times to make sure it really worked. We created "El Nino" by heating the ocean spots. We changed the weather circulation pattern just by heating up the atmosphere. We tried it in New Mexico in the 1960s and killed a lot of sheep on the Hopi and Navajo reservations. We did that. There is an area in the San Luis Valley of Colorado that we call the "war zone." It covers fifty miles of northern New Mexico and fifty miles of southern Colorado. This is where experiments are tried out. Not only by us, but by the extraterrestrial races. The cattle mutilations people hear about are part of these experiments.

Now, I knew there had been UFO contact. The Air Proving Ground Command had been involved in high-level top secret UFO research for years. I had a Top Secret Ultra II Clearance in cryptographics. This means that I was thirty-eight levels above Top Secret. I also had what was called Cosmic Clearance which is even above Ultra II Clearance and deals with aliens. This was the type of work I was doing: I was on the No. 1 team, also known as the Blue Book team, which investigated UFO sightings. I would go, as a military official, and talk to the people who had seen UFOs to convince them that they had not seen anything. If I could not sway them, if they kept on insisting that they saw something, then the No. 2 team would go in. They would threaten their families. If No. 2 team did not do it, then they sent out "OO-Boys." That would be the end of that—in one way or another.

To discover the truth of our extraterrestrial history we can research the available facts. We've had contact with ETs and we've signed treaties. In the future we are going to be able to communicate with a lot of extraterrestrial races. I think that we are going to be guided. If our government does not come out of the system of secrecy, the extraterrestrials will force their hand. What has been kept secret for more than fifty years is beginning to be revealed over the Internet. I feel that the extraterrestrials are the ones who really seeded the Internet. After all, they gave us transistors, they gave us printed circuits, and they gave us anti-gravitational electromagnetic propulsion systems—why not the Internet, too? The Internet can bypass all the power of other forms of media. The aliens are now reaching people through the Internet as well as through dreams, sightings, and transmissions.

Most people who have had communication with ETs have said that it wasn't through words, even though extraterrestrials can speak telepathically. In the cases that I have researched, people who have communicated with extraterrestrials have instead received a "feeling" of great love and understanding. Naturally, some people took the other side, fear. Some people are convinced of things through fear. It shouldn't be that way, but we have gotten used to that process of understanding. Our government does that—tries to convince people through fear; they threaten or put people in jail for falling in their disfavor. I think the extraterrestrials will teach us that locking people up doesn't change them a bit for the good, it makes them worse.

We are living in what I think is the most exciting time in human history on Earth. There is a story of Israel in the Old Testament. The people lived under Judges for years. The Lord did not want to give them a king because a king would take their young men, send them to war, and make them pay taxes. Under the Judges' rule, the taxes were given to the Lord. But because everybody else had a king, the Lord agreed and gave the Israelites King Saul. It happened: the king declared wars. The people supported the king rather than the Lord. It seems that we have come to that point. With the authority and backing of the Supreme Court the Judges have now chosen a new Lord. The President has become the all-powerful king. So maybe we are going back to the Ancient way.

And yet this is an exciting time because we have the capability to realize "paradise." The Andromedans told our government that in their world there is no such thing as money. Everything that everybody needs is supplied. For instance, if you were a doctor, what is important is treating illness, not how much the treatment costs. The same holds true if you were a lawyer; your purpose would be to help people understand the laws. People should know that we have the capability of getting off the petroleum economy.

Currently the oil industry runs the world. But this can change. There is already a Galactic Federation, the UMO-Lyran-Pleiadian-Andromedan-Sirian Confederation, guiding us. Our government signed a limiting treaty with the Zeta Reticuli. This treaty expired in 1997, so nothing stops us from dealing with the higher federation. Nothing except misunderstanding and self-imposed fear. People have become too complacent to research the facts. Instead they strive to maintain the status quo of having a job, a house, and two cars in the garage.

We need to expand our consciousness, to learn and to really immerse ourselves in the history and religion of what we have been taught. Investigate not what Christ, Buddha, and Mohammed *did* but what they *taught*. One thing that people should realize is that we make our tomorrow. Thought is the most important aspect of who we are. In spiritual unity we can create a peaceful tomorrow— 2002 is you!

The Brotherhood of the Snake

A Quest   For the Truth   Upon the Blue Planet

Earth   In a New Age   A New Dimension

Awaiting the Return   Of the Wingmakers

The Gods of Old   The True Brotherhood

Of the Serpent   Wisdom

Lost Cities   UFOs   Visiting Star Ancestors   Create

Mystical Symbols   Of Secret Lodges

Preserving   The Sacred Places   Of an Ancient Race

Students of Light   Inherit Intelligence

Of Extraterrestrial Knowledge   Standing

Side by Side   With the Interplanetary Guardians

Of Our   Solar System

Embrace   The Expanding   Universe

Cells   Of Collective Memory   The Essence

Of Evolution   From   Ancient Records   Spirits

Travel   The Great Path   Of Initiations

A Transmission   A Ceremony

Woven by the Elder Race

Are we a humanoid race fashioned from a global gene pool? Hindu records in the Mahabharata indicate that, a millennium or more before the appearance of Christ, we humans were witnesses to the explorations of ancient astronauts from another star system. Throughout civilization, we are confronted over and over again with tales of space-traveling gods who visited our planet to prepare mankind for a new age of knowledge and wisdom that would come as a consequence of the next evolutionary step. Modern occult secret societies know of these traditions and have always sought ways of communicating with the ancient astronauts like those who arrived in Babylon, India, and Mesoamerica all those centuries ago. We are members of a federation within our own galaxy. The Lirans, the Sirians, the Pleiadians, and the Andromedans are the Watchers who not only jumpstarted our evolution but are awaiting the time when we may be able to take our rightful place in interstellar space.

6 The Geneticists

In Solitude

ANA BRITO
Cuban-Basque Writer and Medium

> *I got a whole volume of the Mahabharata, to pick up everything I could about these "Vimanas" (flying machines) the Ancients had . . . they had been in contact with Space People. The Star People could visit Earth and we could visit the stars.*
>
> LORD DESMOND LESLIE,
> NEPHEW OF SIR WINSTON CHURCHILL

Ana Brito

Tracing her lineage to the Basque region of Spain and the Canary Islands, Ana descends from a long line of wise women. Her paternal great-aunt, Nena Brito, is a gifted medium, and her maternal grandmother, Emma Saenz-Aquero, a great visionary. Exposed to vast storehouses of knowledge since early childhood, Ana is driven by a call to filter higher consciousness to people of all ages and backgrounds. As a writer, Ana is currently working on her first book, Philo & Sophia: Love and Wisdom for the Information Age.

From my own experience and from what I have been taught by my grandparents and ancestors, Cuban spirituality is really a blend of beliefs: Catholicism, in its more traditional form, and Santería. A derivative of the Lucumi religion, Santería was carried to Cuba by slaves taken from West Africa. The African culture blended with the prevailing religion on the island at the time, which was Catholicism. The amalgamation of colonial Catholicism with the saints, entities, gods, and goddesses of the Lucumi faith is what became Santería. *Santería* comes from the word *santos,* which is the worship of saints or deities. God encompasses the master figurehead of the Santería pantheon, but there are also lesser demigods. These have gender, they are the males and the females. For example, the head of the pantheon of saints is Chango, also known as Santa Barbara. Chango is an androgynous entity, both male and female. As the story goes, many hundreds of years ago, during a time of war, a grand estate was on fire. There was a war going on. Chango disguised himself, shape-shifting from male to female, to bypass the soldiers and rescue the people of the estate. There is also Yemaya, who is the goddess of the river, and Ochun, who is the goddess of the ocean. They are both very beautiful females. Ochun dresses in a blue cape with a white dress, and Yemaya has a yellow dress and a blue cape. Yemaya and Ochun both rule over childbirth. If a woman has trouble during labor, one would call on these deities to aid with the birthing.

Columbus first touched land in the Caribbean, and Spanish colonizers soon followed. In Cuba, the Spaniards massacred the indigenous peoples. They waged fierce wars against the Caribe tribe and annihilated the peaceful Hatveys—an agrarian tribe that fished and grew fruits and vegetables. (I have been told that there is a very small Hatvey community that remains and maintains their customs, but most people say that they are gone.) They put captured Indians to work as slaves. The Indians began to die from disease and mistreatment. Their hands were cut off if they did not bring gold from their labor. When they resisted, protesting the labor and mistreatment, they were eliminated. The Spaniards soon began bringing slaves over from Africa. Today, remnants of the indigenous cultures, African slaves, and European colonizers can be seen intermixed throughout the Cuban community. There are Anglo-Cubans with blond hair, light skin, and green eyes, as well as Cubans of dark hair, dark skin, and brown eyes. Cubans who are descended from peoples of the Canary Islands off the coast of Morocco have a Moorish influence, with almond eyes and an Arabic look. Most Cubans are mulattos—a combination of both African and Spanish descent. The faith tradition gravitates more toward African ritual and ceremony.

Witchcraft and voodoo is the dark side of Santería. Healing and curative medicine is the light side. True practitioners of white magic have a tremendous amount of knowledge about the medicinal value of plants and herbs. Faith healing in this tradition can be a powerful cure. When my grandmother was a child, a family member had a swollen foot. It was gangrenous from an infection. They called in a *curandera,* a practitioner of healing. She used a frog, which she prayed over and ran up and down the affected leg. Then the family hung up the frog to dry, to dehydrate. As the frog dried out, the swelling in the affected leg went down until it was completely healed. That was an occasion where an animal was used but herbs are more common. There are also some wonderful baths used in healing. Traditional remedies are designed to clear your aura of negative energies. You can make such a potion on your stovetop. You boil water with the leaves of the paraíso (paradise) tree, which grows in the tropics. Then you put in cleaned-out eggshells and white flower petals from a rose or gardenia. Then you put in a couple of drops of essential oil. Boil all of this, then let it cool off. For three consecutive days you pour this potion over your body, from your neck down, after you bathe. This is how you eliminate negative energy or any bad thoughts which have come your way.

To clear your house of negative entities or energies, you can make a similar potion. Get a bucket of water, drop in some white flower petals for purity, and add a few drops of an essential oil of herbs or flowers. Use this water to clean your house from the back to the front and out the door. Then pour out the water at an intersection. If the petals get onto the floor while you're cleaning you can leave them. Eggshell, called *cascarilla,* is a very protective white magic. Some people even make a cross on the ground with eggshells and rest their feet on top of it to keep them on the good path and clear away any negativity.

Black magic is the other side of Santería—it is a manipulative art, used for love or to hurt another person. To make someone become ill or suffer financial hardship, a person may kill a chicken in that person's name and leave it on his or her front porch, or throw a cursed egg filled with potions and herbs at the house. In black magic, the curse can often bounce back onto the person directing it; I have seen this happen to people who throw curses—they live a tragic existence from one problem to another. You can always protect yourself from black magic by burning candles, evoking entities to protect you, or taking baths. To remove a curse, a *curandera* (female healer) or *curandero* (male healer) should be called.

I once met a ninety-two-year-old Cuban healer who diagnosed illness through the eyes and toenails and treated people with medicinal herbs. He told me about photographs he had taken of the universe while traveling in meditation. With his physical body in a meditative state, he would project his conscious self into space, taking with him a 35 mm camera. He would put the lens to his third eye and take pictures of the planets in our solar system as well as the sun and the moon. He has boxes of these photos. I have seen the pictures, and so has Kodak—they wanted to know where he got them. We don't need contraptions to ascend into space. We can travel as the ancients who traversed the universe, viewing the planets, the galaxy, and the continents of our Earth.

To me the good entities of Santería are much more than saints. An entity is actually any kind of being which inhabits a body, whether it is physical or etheric. There are really entities from all different dimensions and all planetary realms. We live in a dual universe, meaning negative and positive, male and female. Everything becomes what you perceive it to be, and this affects how you deal with that understanding. I consider myself a medium, like the women before me, and so I have had encounters with many entities. In one encounter, in 1993, something woke me from sleep one night. At the foot of my bed I saw a being. It had no features—no eyes. The shoulders were not wide, it was a slender figure, and it looked androgynous. The being was gliding in front of my bed, and it had a muted golden aura around it. I was frozen—paralyzed—as I watched. The being came around me to my left side and stood next to me. I felt it put one hand in my chest on my heart and the other hand on my throat. It seemed to be tuning my chakras. I felt a warm liquid light of unconditional love flow into me, and then I passed out in sleep.

In 1997 I saw a female—a Grey. I hate to call them aliens because they are actually from here. She was standing behind me as I lay in my bed one night. I felt her put her hand in my skull, in my brain, and I felt her pulling something out. The mind can interpret only so much, and if we have no frame of reference for what we see it is hard for us to make sense of it, but to me what she pulled out looked like thirteen individual coils. She could have been connecting or disconnecting something; I'm not entirely sure.

The beings I would identify as Greys are our keepers or guardians. They have a specific mission here. We perceive them as being from outer space, but really they are here on this planet, under the water, inside the earth, in another dimension. They have always been here, for they are the keepers of the DNA. They are what continues to perpetuate and reintroduce humankind to this planet. As keepers of the DNA, they come in at the end of one cycle, the beginning of a new cycle. Earth goes through cycles. We humans experience these cycles as the passing of time, but time is really just cycles, or circles of existence on the planet. At the beginning and end of each cycle, the Greys, these keepers of the DNA, make their presence known. This present cycle, according to one of the Mayan calendars and other predictions, is supposed to end in 2012—soon. That is why so many people are claiming experiences of "alien abduction," and of aliens probing them and performing surgical procedures on them. The keepers are extracting DNA in order to produce a hybrid

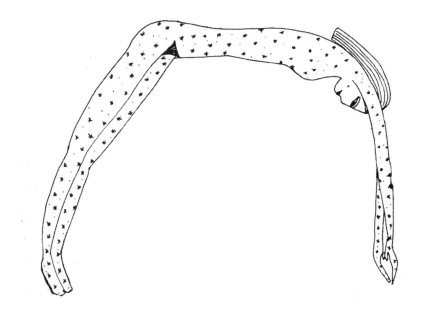

STAR TRAVELER

race that can be reintroduced on the earth plane once the cycle changes. They are extracting DNA from everything—humans, plants, animals, and everything else—that needs to continue into the next world. The cellular makeup of life on this planet—what it was, what it is, and what it will be—is being revealed. The human body is created like the planet, which is created like the solar system, which is created like the galaxy, which, in turn, is created like the universe. Everything is an extension of everything else. All life on this planet begins as one giant strand of DNA. We are all connected. If you were to link up the genetic code of every single consciousness—animal, plant, rock, human—you would have the original undiluted DNA— a physical map and genetic blueprint of the planet. When this DNA was first introduced by the Greys, there were different entry points, through which the root races came to Earth. There were eight entry points, and eight sets of pyramids, of which only five can be found at this time. There were eight DNA bands that came in through these entry points and established the eight root races. Now there are only five left. There is a race anchored in Greenland, for example— a whole civilization buried under the ice from the last cycle—that doesn't look like us. This race will emerge as Greenland thaws.

The extraterrestrials are geneticists. They know that is the role they play in creation. We should learn the role that we should be playing. The extraterrestrials are our ancestors. They are both our past and our future because time is really circular. They are the most evolved beings that can manifest physically and come into this dimension. In other words, they can be seen as creator workers in the physical realm. There is a main source, a Godhead, from which everything emanates. At best we can perceive this Godhead as light, for if we could truly perceive this source we would not be here anymore, we would be the source itself. Our purpose is to evolve and recognize that love is the unifying force and that we are all extensions of that source. We are genetically, spiritually, and energetically linked. We come from each other.

At the end of a cycle Earth experiences major cataclysm. As with any other living being, she will do what she has to do to survive. The Earth survives by washing herself inside out and starting over again. We are in the midst of that purification process. The more environmental damage we subject the Earth to, the more she will have to repair herself. We are involved in the mission of what we see as destruction.

The Maya could project in and out of the cycles, and so they could foretell the future. At some point, however, they could no longer chart the heavens—something had shifted; a new cycle brought a tilt in polar alignment. I believe that the planet will soon again experience a shift in polar alignment. The axis of the planet will shift or tilt, and with that come earthquakes, volcanoes, tidal waves, and other natural disasters at a global level. Imagine the entire planet under hurricane conditions, with global warming melting the polar ice caps, and the ozone disappearing. Coastal regions will be under water; some people may retreat to underground living. There are zones which will be safe havens where there may be oracles or faith areas which will be protected. The rest of Earth, however, will be in chaos. The entire rotation of Earth will change; it will be in a different location in space. Even a relatively small fifteen- to twenty-degree shift will have dramatic results. Our conditions on Earth, the laws of physics, are strictly for this planet. As the planet changes orbit or location in space, the conditions on the planet will also change. Life as we know it will change. This will mark the end of the current cycle. There are really three options for humans at the end of this cycle we are currently experiencing. One third of the planet will remain to repopulate, one third of the planet will die in natural disasters, and one third will ascend into a higher dimension. The Motherships are going to come and pick up a lot of people. There are those who will continue karmic manifestation or, in other words, reincarnate on this planet because they choose to stay—coming to this plane is actually a choice. Some people volunteer to come in order to speed the purification process along. These people are called Lightworkers. Those who ascend will move on to another dimension and become a part of creation. One can be a co-creator in another realm. The whole point of ascension is to not experience a physical death.

In this time of transition, the most important thing to remember is to trust your inner voice; listen to what it tells you and go where it leads you. This voice comes through very subtly—not as a big cloud descending from heaven with trumpets playing but as a glimpse, a little inkling, that unfolds into a greater understanding and vision of your path. You need to go where the energy calls you, tapping into your inner knowledge in order to be where you need to be when the cataclysm occurs. You are recommended to listen to the warning signs, the red indicators that are coming up all over the place telling people to wake up! Get moving. Cities are the worst place to be. In our natural evolution we have been nomadic, making migrations according to the elements of nature. Yet eventually we decided to settle in cities where concrete structures break the flow of natural energy sources with weight and overpopulation in specific areas. We are meant to follow the patterns like the animals do so as not to burn out and contaminate our natural resources in any given area. One consideration is your source of water. When a natural disaster strikes, water is immediately the first element to become contaminated. People will kill each other for a glass of water, and the first thing to go is the water. What do we need to survive, more than anything, if not water?

The New Age, the New Consciousness, is spilling over into past and future worlds. Asking for higher knowledge is a matter of choice. If you ask, it will come; through grace, the universe will give. Finding where you need to be during the cataclysm—that is where faith comes in, faith in the sixth sense. Fear is the instrument used to disempower mankind. The government has used it—through the media—to keep the populace from knowing about our contact with extraterrestrials. The media is the government's tool for reaching the populace. How better to disarm and disorient than to put out frightening disinformation? Bad news sells. But the government can't control the "extraterrestrial problem," as they call it, though they try everything in their power to do just that. People want to hear the truth. The truth is so filtered, dissected, and manipulated that you have to read between the lines in order to hear it.

The truth is that there was a treaty signed, after Roswell, between the government and an extraterrestrial race. The technology of the Stealth Bomber, the flying triangle called the "Manta," the laser, and plasma rays—where do we think these came from? They are from recovered vehicles of extraterrestrial origin. I believe the government will stage a "false" UFO landing to create panic and perpetuate their cover-up. What better way to control and disorient the populace than an alien invasion? Look at *War of the Worlds,* by Orson Welles; this created total panic.

Yet all this government cover-up is really of little consequence to human evolution and our expanding consciousness. We are ascending to another dimension where our capabilities will transcend any government agenda. Once this occurs, there is no need of state, church, or cash. The New World Order and days of Babylon are numbered.

Those who stay in prayer and meditation—the Tibetans, the Hindus, the Kogi—are anchoring the planet to maintain the balance. We should thank those people as we expand and open ourselves to everything within the inner and outer worlds.

In Solitude

In Solitude   We Pray   For Balance
To Restore   The Nations   Of the Earth
To Raise   The Level   Of   Understanding
The Consciousness   Through   The Geneticists
The Keepers   Of the DNA

With an Attitude   Of Service   Respecting
The Process   Mind to Mind   In the Highest Order
Uniting   To Vibrate   With the Possibility
Throughout the Globe

That Elements   Which Bond   In Strength
And Hold Fast   To the Path   Of Peace
Will Purify   The Changing Cycle

The Lyrans   The Sirians
The Pleiadians   The Andromedans
Living   Breathing Beings
The Jumpstarters   Of   Our Evolution
Call Us   To Take   Our Place
In   Interstellar   Space

In America there is another style of transit for freight and passengers, far exceeding rapid transit. Secret underground shuttle networks crisscross every state in the United States on an endless subterranean highway. This network and its checkpoints cross the oceans to become the worldwide network called the subglobal system. Using a mag-lev vacuum method, travel takes place at Mach 2, twice as fast as the speed of sound. Electromagnetic propulsion systems (extraterrestrial reproduction vehicles), cloning, secret projects, underground military bases— they are all more than just science fiction.

7

High Strangeness

Spiritual Choice

JAMES LUJAN
Taos Pueblo Tiwa Filmmaker

> *I challenge you to become personally involved and prove the claims made herein point-by-point, one way or another.*
>
> COMMANDER X, *THE DULCE WARS*

JAMES LUJAN

James Lujan is a thirty-five-year-old filmmaker from Taos Pueblo lands. A graduate of Stanford University and U.S.C. Film School, his first feature documentary, called High Strange, New Mexico, *is about the UFO subculture in his home state. His second documentary,* Little Rock's Run, *concerns Little Rock Reed, an American Indian fugitive. His recently completed documentary,* Inner Spirit, *looks at AIDs in the Pueblo community. James is the founder of Taos Productions, Ltd., Co. and also the Taos Filmmaker's Initiative, which offers workshops, seminars, and a supportive environment for emerging filmmakers. He completed his first dramatic feature,* Of Things Unknown, *a film set in Taos that deals with UFOs, sex, and spirituality. Currently, James' production company is building a digital film and video studio, the only Native American owned film facility to date.*

I always was very interested in film; my parents got me a super-8 camera when I was ten years old. I went to college at Stanford University with the intention of studying medicine. After I took my first chemistry course, I realized that I wasn't cut out for the sciences. I decided to pursue film instead. Stanford had a communications program with film classes, so I majored in communications. After I graduated, I went to U.S.C. Film School in Los Angeles. That is where I learned the nitty-gritty about filmmaking and the film industry. When I had enough of L.A., I moved back to New Mexico. I started to write and freelanced at the Albuquerque Journal. I realized that if I wanted to have a career in film, I would have to make it happen myself. So in 1995 I went out and got film equipment. One of the arts writers at the Journal, Tony Dela Fora, had been thinking about writing a book about the incident at Roswell. He had already pulled together some stories about the UFO industry in New Mexico. His idea was to give bus tours of all the famous UFO sites in New Mexico—Roswell, Socorro, and Dulce. At that time, I was looking to undertake a first film project. . . . I suggested to Tony, "Why not make a ten-minute promotional video to go along with the book?" He said "Sure, why not? Let's do this."

We took our first trip down to Roswell in the fall of '95, around Labor Day. We set up interviews with people at the Roswell UFO Museum. After a few sessions we realized that we had more than a ten-minute book promotion video on our hands. We decided to devote all our energy to the documentary, and the book project fell by the wayside. We spent all our time talking with people about their UFO experiences and networking with the UFO community, starting in Roswell and then all over the state. We heard all sorts of stories about the many incidents that have occurred in New Mexico. After all that research, we concluded that New Mexico is probably one of the most unique places on the planet as far as UFO activity is concerned. It's a definite hot spot. If you think about it,

New Mexico is the only place that boasts all aspects of the UFO phenomenon: crashed UFO craft, government cover-up, underground bases, abductions, cattle mutilations, and so on. Everything seems to happen here. The only phenomenon we haven't found evidence of here is crop circles.

Our research became my first film. *High Strange, New Mexico* is basically a collection of interviews. Most UFO documentaries approach the subject from a very scientific point of view. They go in trying to prove or disprove this person's sighting or theory. We knew that we could never prove or disprove anything. We went in with the attitude of just wanting to hear people's stories—and they have fascinating stories to tell. We

HIGH STRANGE, NEW MEXICO

thought that there might be a common denominator among all the sightings and all the stories. What grew out of the documentary is the fact that the ancient Spanish and Indian cultures of New Mexico make it a place of great knowledge and spiritual energy, which lends itself to the population's fascination with UFO phenomena. That ancient spiritual energy is one of the reasons people are attracted to the Southwest, whether or not they realize it. And when you are looking for God or the meaning of life, you look up to the sky. What do you see there? UFOs!

Or the government. One of the more sinister aspects of the film is the uncovering of the government's role in the UFO phenomenon. The government manipulates people's beliefs—either against them or as a cover story—to throw a smoke screen around its own activities; it is called spreading misinformation. One of our interviewees, Jim Marrs, gives some insight into the government's

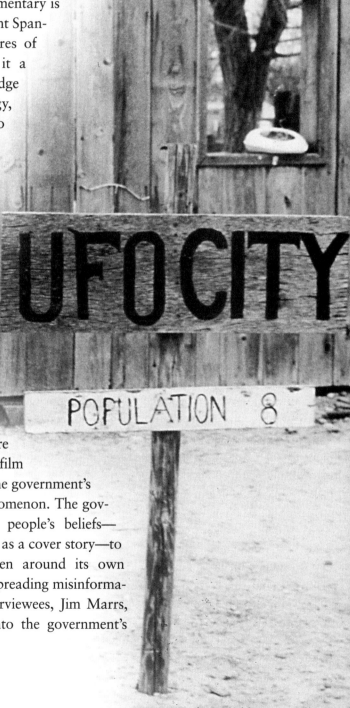

role. He is the author of *Alien Agenda* and *Crossfire,* the J.F.K. story on which Oliver Stone partially based the movie *J.F.K.* Jim Marrs commented that part of the problem with the UFO phenomenon is not that there isn't enough information but that there's too much. We have so much varying information about UFOs that it clogs up and blurs the line between reality and fiction, which in turn leaves us unable to agree on the true facts concerning the aliens, the Greys, or the cosmic New Age vision. Through Jim Marrs, we found some interesting parallels between UFOs and the J.F.K. assassination concerning government cover-ups and the suppression of evidence. President Kennedy wanted to make some of this UFO information available to the public—this was his intention. In *Rule by Secrecy* Jim Marrs investigates the modern day secret societies and the suspicious ways in which they conceal the UFO truth and orchestrate history—the drugs, the wars, the media, the stock market, and the oil industry—keeping humanity out of the loop. That is the mission of the New World Order of International Bankers, to keep humanity out of the loop. Now we have Bush, who has all the ties to the CIA, the Illuminati, the shady oil and drug dealings. It's all documented. We have Clinton tied to cocaine smuggling in Arkansas and sex in the Oval Office; all this stuff adds to the mix of suspicion.

By the time we had finished with *High Strange, New Mexico,* we had shot almost fifty hours of interviews, all independently financed. Needless to say, we had a lot of material, and not all of it made it into the final cut. One of the segments that we cut was about Sandia Laboratories and their experiments with particle rays. According to our interviewee, Sandia Labs is experimenting with particle ray tests on "metallic matter." Our contact would not say exactly what these metals were, but he indicated that they were of extraterrestrial origin. In some of the experiments, the particle beams made the metallic matter disappear. This frightened our contact, because no one was supposed to be conducting that type of experiment and these actions had to be accounted for. Where the materials disappeared to, no one knows.

We also interviewed Norma Milanovich, who was employed at Sandia Labs. She wrote a book, *We, The Arcturians,* in which she claims to be in contact, through a computer, with extraterrestrials whom she calls elevated masters. Milanovich is not someone you can dismiss easily, for she worked at Sandia Laboratories with a high "Q" clearance. Sandia knew about her claims, but evidently she was able to balance her professional duties with her interest and contact with extraterrestrial beings. There is an actual clip in the film where we have her making contact with these ascended masters. In the film she also made interesting reference to the three highest points of spiritual energy on the planet. One is in the Himalayas, one is in Peru, and one is here in northern New Mexico; taken together, they form an equilateral triangle.

We first heard about activities at Dulce, New Mexico, through another one of our contacts, who told us to talk with Gabe Valdez, a former New Mexico State Police officer in the Dulce area. The town of Dulce is close to the Colorado border and situated on the Jicarilla Apache Indian Reservation. We were told that Valdez had some interesting stories about alien activity and secret government underground bases. At the same time we heard about Paul Bennewitz, UFO investigator, physicist, and president of Thunder Scientific Labs, which is adjacent to Kirkland Air Force Base. Bennewitz is a physicist-scientist who has developed equipment for NASA's space shuttles and several Fortune 500 companies. He claims that, while working on electronic instruments, he received transmissions from an alien collective via a radio-video link to the underground extraterrestrial base at Dulce. Bennewitz was heavily involved with Project Beta—a scientific study of alien intervention and electronic surveillance in association with the Dulce underground military facility—and with a man named Philip Schneider, an ex-government structural engineer who was involved in building underground military bases around the country.

We filmed an interview with Philip Schneider, and in that segment, which turned out to be his last lecture before he was murdered, he actually predicted his own death. He talks about

surviving a military encounter that took place at the underground facility at Dulce between our government and the aliens.

He was part of a government team of engineers that was digging out the mountain for the tunneling system of the underground base. He claimed that during the course of that dig the team came across an alien station and there was a big gunfight, in which he was wounded. Since then Schneider has devoted his life to spreading the news about the aliens. His father was Captain Oscar Schneider of the United States Navy, who worked in nuclear medicine and helped design the first nuclear submarines. Schneider claimed that his father was involved with the Philadelphia Experiment.

All of this was the background information that Tony and I had before we took our trip up to Dulce in 1996. Gabe Valdez had generously offered his time to us, and he showed us around town. He talked about the old days when he was head of the State Police and how the cops used to chase the orange and blue balloon-shaped lights in the sky. He would receive calls from scared cops, and then they would go and chase these lights all over Dulce. I don't think he understood the history or the ramifications of what was going on until he moved to Albuquerque and met Paul Bennewitz. They met in the late 1970s, and since Valdez had spent so much time observing events in Dulce and Bennewitz was very interested in the UFO/government activity there, they began feeding each other information about their experiences. Bennewitz told Valdez that there was a secret underground base at Dulce and that the aliens and the government were working together. He also told him that there was an uneasy alliance and truce between the two. There was some kind of deal in which the government was allowing cattle mutilations, but only a certain number of them. Valdez took his family and Bennewitz out to Dulce. They camped out at Mount Archuleta to see if they could observe anything in the sky. I spoke with Valdez's wife and his grown children who told me that they saw blue streaks

THE BEING
by Lorne Honyumptewa

of lights heading toward Mount Archuleta, almost as if the lights were going to crash into it. Then the lights just faded into the mountain. For them, this experience was pretty wild. They went back another time because Valdez was accompanying Dr. John Gille, a French scientist, to see whether there was continued activity and to identify the craft entering the base as alien craft or government craft. Somewhere in the course of their trip they were stopped by a black helicopter; it descended and men dressed in black uniforms came out and physically removed them from the mountain. They were pretty traumatized by that, and Valdez was convinced that something suspicious was afoot. Even if the lights they saw were a mass hallucination, the removal by the government team certainly was not.

Some time later, Bennewitz was working near Sandia Labs. Computers then were still in their infancy, nowhere near as advanced as they are now. They had just a small screen with white numerals or letters—no graphics. One day Bennewitz called up Valdez and said that he was receiving transmissions from aliens via his computer. Valdez claims that he went over to Bennewitz's house and actually saw on the computer screen a reptilian-like creature with what looked like a Roman helmet. Things got progressively weirder from there, and Bennewitz got more and more paranoid. It's possible that the people from Sandia Laboratories were setting him up—feeding him information and sending him transmissions to make him seem like a nut and discredit him. Eventually his paranoia pretty much incapacitated him.

Back to Gabe Valdez and our first trip to Dulce. One night he drove us around Mount Archuleta, which is where the entrance to the base is. We spent a good three or four hours driving around in pitch darkness on the mountain. We were hoping that, at the very least, if we were going too far into the mountain we might get stopped by government agents, which could have indicated that we were going where we weren't supposed to go. But the only weird thing that happened I didn't even see, because I was in the backseat with the camera equipment. Tony and Valdez were up front, and the

Range Rover was going up the mountain. Suddenly Valdez pulled to the side of the road. Tony asked him, "Is it coming yet?" Gabe replied, "No." What they had seen was a pair of headlights. Gabe had pulled to the side of the road to let the vehicle pass. It never came, and when we drove up a little further there was no evidence of a vehicle. Aside from that, we didn't see anything.

Dulce itself struck me as a little town with a big secret. It's a reservation town, and there really isn't much out there except for a Best Western hotel and some small homes for the Apache community. However, Dulce is the place from which cattle mutilations gained such notoriety; many cattle mutilations occurred there in the late 1970s. In fact, it was so rampant that one of the state senators had pushed for an official investigation. The point is, whether or not the legend of Dulce and the secret underground alien base is true, the cattle mutilations happened. There is documented physical evidence. People there seem to be cold to outsiders, especially journalists; I think that is because they were burned by the press, who reported on the situation like the news was coming from crackpots.

Around that time I was also ghostwriting an autobiography for an ex-military intelligence officer who lives in Albuquerque. He is a Hispanic man who grew up in Jemez Springs and has always had a good rapport with Native Americans. He was one of the first people from the class of 1946 to be recruited for the spy program being implemented at that time. He went through all this training, from gas chamber experiments to mind control and other strange things intended to create super soldiers. Because he was of Hispanic descent, he was stationed in South America, where it was thought that he could blend in with the population and hunt down escaped Nazis. At one point he was stricken with malaria and near death. He narrowly recovered and was nursed back to health by one of the Amazon tribes. He said that the tribe's people communicated with him telepathically and that they were able to move through time and space without having to walk. He thought this was amazing—uneducated but nonetheless spiritually advanced people had the ability to travel interdimensionally. The rest of his life story deals with a lot of unsavory aspects of the government in the early days of his service. He talked about the government inflicting environmental terrors by dumping germs and biological agents into big cities in order to see how it would affect the population. These are touchy subjects that are hard to substantiate with documentation. There is some information on the Internet, but again it's hard to figure out what's true and what's not—and some of it may be misinformation put out by the government, just to cloud the waters even more. The telepathic abilities of South American Indians is definitely something to be explored. I often hear, within the UFO community, that, drawing from the ancient Mayan calendar, the time predicted for this—the apocalyptic showdown—is 2012. I think this will be the time of a spiritual turning point. I don't doubt that soon we will experience a major spiritual crisis.

When we first started delving into the Native American aspect, we found that the UFO phenomenon reaches far beyond the past fifty years. Most Native American cultures want their creation stories to be known, and most creation stories start with the Star Ancestors and beings from other realms.

Through all the experience of making *High Strange, New Mexico* and all the networking with the UFO community, I never saw a spacecraft or any physical sign of aliens. However, I did come away with a real sense of spiritual intensity. I feel that we should find our own spiritual path and be decisive about it. It comes down to personal belief, to what you truly believe in. What bothers me about society today is the hypocrisy—people say they believe in one thing, but they do another. If we do not come to an apocalyptic point in 2012, what will really be important is for each of us to make a spiritual choice for ourselves, and to stay on that path.

Spiritual Choice

Herein Lies   A Spiritual   Choice
At   The Turning Point   Of Critical Mass   Moving
Toward   2012   Changing   The   Physical Path
Of this Planet

The Light   Stays   On the Path   Be Decisive
Receive Transmissions   Of a Higher Nature
Become   Personally Involved   Uncover
The UFO   Phenomenon

Challenge   The Claims   To Prove
Or Disprove   The History   Of Contact
Point by Point   One Way   Or Another

High   Strangeness   Population 8
A   UFO City   An Entrance
Waiting   For Visitors
Go Toward   A   Detective Story
Research   The Facts
Of Your Own   Evolution

The symbols, teachings, and technology from the ancient world have been, and continue to be, used among secret societies in the modern world. The Brotherhood—this global web of secret societies—was and is supported by a phenomenal amount of technological genius. Humanity, for the most part, has been left out of advanced scientific spirituality. The esoteric teachings of the secret doctrines of the Knights of Templar, the Illuminati, the Freemasons of High Degree, the Brothers of the Rose Cross, and other "underground" orders have hoarded ancient texts to rewrite history. In the Brotherhood and within their symbols, it is clearly stated, "we control all that is just, all that is right, all that is fair." As the veil of dark shadows lifts, the truth is being revealed that contact with ancient extraterrestrial races has occurred. Knowledge of this will allow mankind to take its rightful place in interstellar space.

8

Guardians of the Gate

Women's Earth Wisdom

COLLEEN KELLY
Scottish-Irish Women's Leader

It is said that the influence can come in two different ways. If they come from the East, they will come slowly and bring with them wisdom which people will need. If they are not accepted by the people, then they will come from the West. There will be a big population. They will come to control this land, and will swarm all over it in just one day! We were instructed not to resist them, when they come, for they will have no mercy for anybody.

DAVID MONONGYE, HOPI ELDER,
HOLDING TO THE PATH OF PEACE

COLLEEN KELLY

Colleen is cofounder of Living Systems, an organization that provides training for communication skills and conflict resolution for small businesses and entrepreneurs. She is codirector of the Women's Alliance, a program designed to empower women. Colleen is nationally recognized as a community leader; she has been featured in Visionary Voices: Women on Power *and has appeared on* Good Morning, America. *Colleen leads wilderness treks in Nepal and works with Sacred Arts, an organization formed to study wisdom traditions from around the world. She is a talented artist, and her works have been exhibited around the globe. Colleen Kelly has been practicing Tibetan Buddhism for over twenty years.*

When I was four or five years old, my family lived in Chicago. My parents were practically kids. My mother worked nights as a nurse; my father went to medical school and also worked at a gas station. We lived in a small trailer behind that gas station. It had one bedroom; that was where my parents slept. It also had a kitchen and a living room with a couch; that's where I slept. Sometimes I would be awakened in the middle of the night by an apparition of a man standing by my bed. I could see him very clearly. He was murky brown in color, almost khaki, and he smelled bad. He would say, "I want to speak to your father." When I had strange visions like this, I would wake up my folks. They thought that I was having nightmares. In some cases, I was. They would come out and tell me that they didn't see anything, that I must have been dreaming. Then they would often let me sleep with them. I did not know at the time that this was my grandfather. My mother had left her family and I had never met him—besides, he was dead long before I was born.

One day a few years later, when I was seven, I asked permission to go to the cinema. Neither of my parents could take me and, since they were raising me to be independent, they let me go alone. It wasn't very far. But something terrible happened. A man came and sat down next to me in the theater. He took my hand, and then he kidnapped me. We were sitting in his car, and he was reaching for me, probably to rape me and maybe kill me, when I realized that I was in extreme danger. Suddenly this huge ball of light appeared from my chest and struck the man over his heart. I could see this light; it was a beautiful color and it made this man cry. He began to sob, and he let go of me. He hung his head and yelled at me to get out of the car. I did, and I ran really fast all the way home.

My parents had always told me never to go anywhere with strangers, so why I went with this particular man was a mystery. But years later, I did hypnosis work around this incident. I learned that the stranger who kidnapped me had reminded me of the man who appeared near my bed at night when I was a small child. Just recently I did some more work around this incident with a woman who is a healer. What came out was that my dead grandfather, who had committed suicide, had been the intervening force, the beautiful ball of light, in that kidnapping. He actually saved my life, as a guardian figure. During my work with the healer I received a really powerful feeling that he had seen the harm that his suicide had done to my father. In saving me, he made atonement for what he had done.

Around the time of the kidnapping incident, my folks sent me to a Catholic school—for the education, not because they were interested in my becoming a Catholic, though the nuns and priests certainly did try to convert people. I was drawn to the stories of the saints, the stories of Jesus healing people, and the visionary experiences that were a part of people's life at that time. I had already seen what most people call ghosts or spirits. I felt very at home with the idea that there were other realms and beings that one could communicate with. I converted to Catholicism for a few years but left the Church by the age of thirteen. Catholic iconography and symbols still appear from time to time in my artwork.

When I was a teenager, I had a series of out-of-body experiences. I would go to sleep and the next thing I knew, I'd be in other worlds, other realms. I was aware of being out of my body and looking down; I could see things that were actually happening. This made me curious. The experience was very strong and seemed to have a connection to my wanting and receiving information.

In my family, there was always a certain amount of openness about the extraordinary and the supernatural. My mother was quite psychic—she had visionary and prophetic dreams. My father was very interested in Theosophy and brought home books by Madame Blavatsky, such as *The Secret Doctrine* and *Isis Unveiled,* which led to the open atmosphere around extraordinary and supernatural phenomena. He also was very interested in extraterrestrials. He was convinced that he himself was a Venusian, from the White Star, and that he didn't belong here on Earth. He used to say that he was going back. As a child I would move my bed so that I could look at the stars before I went to sleep. I, too, had a feeling that I came from somewhere else out there in the cosmos. I wanted to stay connected to the Star People. My father bought land in San Geronimo, in northern California, and built a log cabin in the redwoods. One time he took me out to a clearing behind the house and said, "See, it's just perfect for flying saucers. They are coming to get me!"

My father had numerous books on sightings, and he was always combing bookstores for more. Some of the sightings we read about dated back several hundred years. One that I recall in particular happened during the landing of the Pilgrims. It's incredible—there are actually documented records of UFO phenomena in North America as far back as the 1600s.

What happened to Native Americans also occurred to the tribes of Europe. The decimation of these tribes was partly due to the Spanish Inquisition, but the Spanish weren't the only ones responsible. Millions of people were killed and a very large number of these people were women. These women were the keepers of the wisdom tradition, and they were killed because of it. Sometimes whole villages were completely wiped out. A wave of horror swept through Europe and eradicated all of these Earth traditions. Wisdom was lost and had to be hidden. The same beliefs that caused the persecution of Europe's Earth traditions came to North America and, in a way, still sweep around the world. At this very moment in Tibet, there are whole villages and tribal peoples who, with this massive wave of industrial force, have been displaced. . . . Yet people are now coming forth with the Celtic traditions. When one hears these traditions it is understandable how the Indians and the Irish got together in this country and why there is so much intermixing between these cultures.

I have been thinking a lot about the recovery of the Earth traditions and how it occurs. I practice Tibetan Buddhism. As a Buddhist practitioner I believe in reincarnation and karmic consequences. There are some subjects in the Tibetan tradition, similar to the Native American, that you just don't talk about—the secret inner teachings of the Tibetans have a circle of protection around them. I sometimes receive knowledge from my study of Aikido. In the process of studying Aikido, I, within my inner world, asked the founder of Aikido how I could know about the inner teachings. This man who founded Aikido was a Shinto Master, connected to the nature spirits. He told me to go study with Native American medicine people. As a result, I started to do sweat lodge and go into solo wilderness vision quest. I met the Indian people to guide me in this journey.

Another thread of information comes from being around teachers who in reality have an extraordinary relationship to the elements and with nature. I met a Tibetan teacher named Ngapa (wandering Yogi) Yeshe Dorje (Thunderbolt) whose wisdom is connected to the crystal. He had been a wandering yogi, meaning that he had made the rounds of the Tibetan *charnel grounds.* These are the places where the bodies of the dead are cut up and offered to the birds and the wild beasts for sky burials. In Tibet you can't bury the dead because the ground is frozen and you can't cremate them because of the high altitiude and lack of firewood. It is common for yogis to practice *chod,* a practice of detaching from the body and ego in order to remedy bad karma and ease the suffering of beings in other

TIBETAN PRAYER

realms, at the charnel grounds. There are 108 charnel grounds—the same number that makes up the beads on a Tibetan rosary. My teacher had done chod three times and became a very powerful teacher. Ngapa Yeshe Dorje had become a very powerful weather controller. He could pacify hailstorms, for instance, which is actually an occupation in Tibet. Through various kinds of practices, they develop the power to pacify storms. This is a really important function in a place where it is very hard to grow food and one hailstorm could wipe out an entire community's food supply. So one of the things my teacher did was this practice. After fleeing from Tibet he became the weather controller for the Dalai Lama. I studied with him for many years. They say that once you start on this path there is no turning around. It is compared to a snake going into a pipe—you can't back out. The only way through is straight ahead.

It is very helpful to have a teacher in order to know where you are in your practice. That is why Guru Yoga—the disciplined relationship between you and a teacher—is so prominent in certain parts of Tibetan Buddhism. Through Guru Yoga your mind stream and the mind stream of the teacher become the same through the practice of devotion. In the Tibetan tradition they say that you connect profoundly with a teacher because of a pre-existing karmic connection.

In Tibetan Buddhism you're also meditating in various ways and one thing builds on another. There is what they call "view," and one of those views is to view the whole world as the deity. All sounds are the sounds of the deity, all manifestations are the manifestations of the deity.

People do not necessarily meet someone who teaches them the traditions—they start in other ways. Some people seem to dream it. For me, it began to show up in my paintings—and then I would develop it. For instance, I had been receiving a recurring image of a white raven; it was quite compelling. I used it first in a drawing and then in a painting. I wondered, "What is this white raven? Where does this image come from?" I wasn't sure, but I thought that one day I would find out. And I did. In Celtic lore, White Raven is the door opener for the days of the dead, known as Samhain. This holiday occurs at the end of October and the beginning of November. It is the time when the veil between the worlds is thin and the dead are able to cross over and visit. The White Raven is Guardian of the Gate between the two worlds. That was my vision. So, the Earth wisdom arises even when there is not a specific person who comes to teach it.

In the early 1970s I became very interested in the ceremonial traditions of the Southwest and so I moved to New Mexico. It was a difficult time in my life. I had become spiritually cynical; I had come to believe that religion was a crutch and that the institution of organized religion bred hatred and war. But then I came across a book by Gina Cerminara called *Many Lives, Many Loves*. It was about the psychic Edgar Cayce, whom I had never heard of. After reading this book, I felt liberated. It was a true epiphany, and I became reconnected with my spiritual life. At the time I was working in a trading post in Old Town Albuquerque. The morning after reading the book, I was opening the shop. It was a great morning, with a midsummer storm coming in. There was nobody else around. All of a sudden this very tall man opened the door and came inside. He was very shy. and he walked around the shop for a while with his head down. Finally he looked up at me and said, "You know a lot about Edgar Cayce!" I was shocked and I quickly looked to see if I had put the book on the counter—perhaps he had spotted it. But it wasn't there. I was bewildered. The man told me that he was a friend of Edgar Cayce, and Edgar had told him to tell me that everything was going to be all right. He said, "I do readings for people, too. I don't have time now, but you must know that everything is going to be all right!" Then he turned and left. This was especially odd because Edgar Cayce was no longer alive. Later I saw a photograph of Edgar Cayce and, strangely enough, he and the man who appeared in the shop looked like the same person. It was a very powerful experience and put me firmly back on a spiritual path.

I began a career as a painter and soon came to feel that this medium was a doorway to other worlds. I began to have experiences at night again. Sometimes, in the middle of the night, I would see a luminous figure. At first it was frightening. It seemed like a man; his hand would come out, and there would be an incredibly high-pitched sound. Then this figure would appear and come forward to touch me. It was similar to the visits I had experienced as a child except that this figure was emanating light. I decided to do a new painting, which I called *Return of the Ghost Dancers*. The Ghost Dance was a dance of renewal and regeneration intended to bring back a world that was fast disappearing. I wanted the painting to have a raw, rather than refined, quality. I stretched a very large canvas on the floor of my studio and painted it there. The painting seems to have something to do with memories. A lot of the symbology in it has to do with the return of the animals, the return of the world that had been lost. It also represented communication with those that had died. I had a relationship with spirit figures and this painting embraced that. During this time, an owl would come to me; it would appear at dusk when I watered the plants. The owl would hover over me and late at night it would actually tap on the windows of my bedroom. The owl is a visitor from the other side, traveling between worlds.

I had another experience once when I spent a week out in Choco Canyon. This was before kivas had been made off-limits to the public, so one evening at sunset I went down into the large kiva at Casa Rinconada, in Choco Canyon, to sit quietly. As I sat there, in my inner world I began to see a blue female hummingbird. There also were lines of women, like a procession of a medicine society. They seemed very old. I eventually created a painting based on that vision, which I called *Blue Medicine*. The image in the painting felt to me like it was connected to migrations, walkabouts, and some kind of very powerful and mysterious ancient time. I later found out that Blue Hummingbird was similar to a mythic being that was connected with Choco Canyon and had somehow been responsible for the people going on what could be called a walkabout.

I have always been very drawn to the mystic quality of the desert. The area's vastness had entered me. I would take journeys by car around the Southwest. One time, as I passed through Hopiland, I heard a man named Richard Castle speak for the Hopi Elders. He was putting out a really fine newsletter which was coming from the

Hopi Elders, trying to bring forth Prophecy so that people could correct the way we were heading. I felt that the intentions of the newsletter were powerful and that it carried an important message. I visited the Hopi for some ceremonies and actually had the opportunity to camp. Richard and I were the only Anglos that I could see—at that time the Hopis did not allow outside visitors onto the reservation. At one dance, it was so hot that I had to sit down, and I found myself next to an old woman. I was doing my best to be very polite, trying to be respectful and to blend in. The drum started, the dancers came out, and this old woman turned to me and spoke about the drum. I responded by agreeing that it was all very exciting. She said, "It gets you, right in here!" And she started rubbing me over my womb. Her eyes sparkled at me. They were really piercing—fierce and friendly at the same time. I laughed with her, and she indicated that I should come and visit her sometime.

That experience stayed with me, and about a month later, I passed through Hopiland again. I arose in the morning and prayed: If we should meet, we will, and if we don't, we don't. It was still quite early when I arrived at the Hopi Cultural Center. Way off in the distance, just on the horizon, I could see a little purple dot. Everything else was very flat. I drove toward it, and soon I could see that it was a person—and it was her! She was standing by the road. When I stopped, she got in the car, and the first words out of her mouth were, "Oh, yeah, I saw you coming from a long way off. I knew you were coming!" By that time my mind was just blown—I could hardly drive. So, Grandmother told me to go to the post office, and on the way we passed a big broad expanse that reached out into the desert. She pointed at it and said, "That's where they come, right there." I asked her, "What?" I was already rattled by the power of her just being there. I asked, "Who comes there?" And she told me, "The UFOs. We see them all the time, we know about them, we've known about them for a long time!" I was barely able to drive the car at that point, but that was all she would say about it.

Women's Earth Wisdom

Women   The Teachers   Holders
Of Inner   And Outer   Passages
Retreats   Of Mythic Beings   Collective
Voices   Safely   Guiding   Us Home

Earth Lodge   Teachings   Traditions
For Discovery   Prepare Us   For the Journey
Of Transformation   Women   Renew
The Beauty Way

Planetary Wisdoms   Roots   Of a Wilderness
Experience   Gather Together
To Embrace   Each Other   And Join
Hands and Hearts

Guardians   Of   The Gate
Visionary   Voices   Study
The   Wisdom Traditions
From   Around   The World.
The Supernatural   Secret Doctrines

There are two different forms of reality: particle and wave. Waves are nonphysical forms, not limited by the confines of this or any other universe. The pineal system of the human brain, including the pineal gland, which is located at the "third eye," has the ability to convert waves into particles, producing particle patterns—pictures, views, configurations—in accord with one's holographic belief systems. This is the science behind manifestation and meditation. We, as human beings, have this unique ability. We can create our own tomorrow. Now energy systems are speeding up and we are moving into higher frequencies. Our DNA and RNA structures are changing—we are ascending as five new frequencies of light—recognized by science—arrive to the Earth plane. At the close of 2012, we will be immersed by light, and there will appear a seventh and most powerful sense of the human instrument—the sense that is linked to time travel which in turn is linked to space travel. The purpose of the Aquarian Perspective Interplanetary mission is to usher in the Age of Light and educate humanity on the Teachings of extraterrestrials to promote omniversal Peace and to practice unconditional love.

Twin Hearts

Star Soul Attunement

DR. RA-JA DOVE
German-Yugoslavian Naturopathic Physician, and

DR. MOI-RA DOVE
Filipino Professor of Philosophy and Ethics

> *The Ancients knew that before the present sky
> and earth were formed, man was already created
> and life had manifested itself four times.*
> IMMANUEL VELIKOVSKY, WORLDS IN COLLISION

RA-JA DOVE AND MOI-RA DOVE

Dr. RA-Ja worked for more than a decade as a naturopathic physician, teaching in medical universities and hospitals and working with chiropractors and doctors while maintaining his own clinics in remote centers around the globe. Professor Moi-RA is the niece of Juan Ortega, the originator of the world-famous Philippine Psychic Surgery center, Union Espiritista Christiana de Filipinas. Following in his footsteps, she is a professor of philosophy, ethics, and religions of the Far East at the University of Manila. Together, Dr. RA-Ja and Professor Moi-RA are cofounders of the Aquarian Perspectives Interplanetary Mission, an organization devoted to aligning spiritual teaching centers with power vortexes around the planet.

Dr. RA-Ja Dove: At a very early age, I began to have psychic experiences, and so I have always believed in spirits, angels, beings from other dimensions. I came of age in the 1960s, when across much of the country there was a great dissatisfaction with what we called the status quo or the governmental establishment. There was also an influx of teachings from the Far East—Hinduism, Buddhism, yoga—that were making inroads into American culture, as well as a renewal of appreciation for the ancient ways of the Native Americans. It was a time of big change for the country.

Some years later I came across the Rainbow Prophecy, which had foretold this time. It predicted that there would come to pass a time when the children of the race of Europeans, who overtook the land, would be reborn into the indigenous cultures of the world, to be mixed as the colors of the rainbow. And these children would rebel against the usurpers of this country. This merging of cultures—those from the East, the Native Americans, the African-Americans, all the oppressed peoples of color—would unite with the hippies, the people of the sixties. The fulfillment of this prophecy generated great idealism; many people believed that all cultures should be able to get along in peace and love. I was brought up to believe in this idealism, but somehow even that did not satisfy me.

I very much wanted an alternative lifestyle, and not to become just another successful businessman. The best thing that I could do with my life was to be of service to others. Through the Great Spirit or Godhead I took up natural healing and dedicated my life to the principles of what would be best for humanity. I had found that Western medicine had been corrupted by money. It had become greed and profit oriented. So I was led to natural healing, naturopathy—a system of healing that treats illness with natural elements from Earth and spiritual methods—no drugs and no invasive procedures. Naturopathy also includes meditation, color healing, and eating the right foods. All these different forms of treating illness began coming together as an Aquarian synthesis, which is what the Age of Aquarius is all about. I became very excited by this and traveled all over the world to study with great natural physicians such as Dr. Bernard Jensen, Dr. R. Christopher, and Dr. Pavvo Airola. They were pioneers of holistic and natural healing. I studied naturopathic practices and techniques in various centers around the world. I received a degree in naturopathy, got a license, and began my practice in Alabama. For a while I found satisfaction there, helping people and being of value in their lives. However, eventually I began to feel that something was missing. I felt like a slave, a robot to the system. I would show up for work every day, and the same twenty to thirty people would show up with the same problems they had had the previous week. Instead of taking responsibility for their own life and health, people only wanted a doctor to heal them. Again, the system of politics within the social custom was making them sick. They ate improper foods, thrived on anger and hate, fought for money and power, and it made them sick. What good was I doing by putting a bandage on a sickness I couldn't heal? The whole point of naturopathy is to get to the cause of the illness, not to heal the symptoms. I threw up my hands to the Great Spirit and said, "Lead me to where life can be of value and life can be worthwhile."

The spirits moved me to give everything away. By the time I was ready to do this I was living in Boston in the ashram of Yogi Amrit Desai, at the Kripalu Foundation, training their medical doctors and staff in iridology. I left everything, got on a ten-speed bicycle, and rode all the way to Central America. Sometimes I would hop on a train or a bus for a thousand or so miles, with the bicycle checked as my baggage, then I'd get off and ride a couple hundred miles. The Great Spirit led me down to Central America where the Mayan pyramids are; it is a land and people still untouched by the civilized monster—I could get next to the land and spirits and receive the truths I was seeking.

In New Gales, I met a crazed-looking white man. He was a CIA agent who told me that I would be shot and killed if I went to Chiapas and Guatemala. He said that the CIA did not want anyone to know what the government was doing to the peoples of Central America. They were instigating a war and did not want any smart white hippie guys, like me, down there telling the people the truth. I recited the Twenty-third Psalm and told him that the Lord would watch over me. Not the false Lord that the business world has created, nor the church teachings of fundamental bigots and war-like militant Christians who kill people of color. The teachings do not say "Love thy Christian neighbor." They say "Love thy neighbor—everybody!" In any case, this man was just an obstacle in the path. Earlier, back in the United States, I had heard about the CIA's war against the indigenous people of Central America. At that time, I felt that it did not really concern me. But why didn't it concern me? We are the sons and daughters of the men who are creating the wars. My adoptive father was a military man. He was a prisoner of war who walked the death march at Bataan. I respected him. I was taught in school that America was a great and beautiful country. The Statue of Liberty says, "Give me your tired, your poor, your huddled masses yearning to breathe free, the wretched refuse of your teeming shore. Send these, the homeless, tempest-tossed, to me. I lift my lamp beside the golden door." I thought that America was a land of acceptance and opportunity for all. I did not know that this was a lie but when I witnessed the problems for the native Mayans in Central America I saw the truth firsthand. The guy was right; they did try to kill me in Central America. I ended up just being removed instead, but I went right back again. I had a mission, and it did not have to do with the CIA. My mission had to do with the Pleiades. At Palenque, in southern Chiapas, I received my instructions intuitively from the extraterrestrials and was told that, in the near future, the Star Ancestors are coming back and some of them will be in human form. Through synchronicity I was given a book with a chapter in it written by Dr. Hunt Lewis Williamson, *Other Tongues, Other Flesh*. I read a particular passage which stood out for me:

"The Knights of the Solar Cross have a highly developed pineal body, or gland, a 'third eye,' which gives them their astounding telepathic abilities. They examine everyone by this 'eye' instead of by normal vision, which would only allow for reason and logic instead of truth." The Knights of the Solar Cross are wandering extraterrestrial beings whose task is to clean up backward worlds. When I had this amazing extraterrestrial experience at Palenque I did not know how to make heads or tails of it. When I read further I discovered that there are many people here on Earth who don't belong here. The Knights of the Solar Cross are the "chimney sweeps"of Creation and it is their specific job to go to the "trash cans" of the Universe and give aid to their fellow beings in the backward worlds. This began to make sense to me. The passages within the book explained the vision I had at Palenque and my mission on Earth. I began naming my work Aquarian Perspectives Interplanetary Mission and gave it the symbol of a spacecraft with wings and a halo, something that all cultures can understand.

Through this extraterrestrial experience I was told to go back to America to write books and articles and spread the word about the mission and the extraterrestrials. This is my life, the truth of my being: to uphold the good of the traditional cultures because they loved living. What more can we do than collect the teachings and give them out? We are not the Great Teachers of the world—we are the runners and the wanderers of the world.

I was guided to go from Yucatán to a Rainbow gathering at Mount Shasta, in California. After the gathering I took teachings and UFO films around to different societies to share the knowledge. I called on the Theosophical Society in Oakland, and there I met its president, Moi-RA, who became my wife. Since then, we have worked together for more than twenty years to share the message of the extraterrestrials, that they are coming to help and bring peace to the planet. We have traveled all over the world, working with the grid lines. We are working in very scientific and technical ways to advance the consciousness of the human species. We are working with the human energy system to upgrade the DNA patterns, using

EASTERN MEDICINE
by Dorit Bat Shalom

extraterrestrial energies and codons. "Codon"is a technical word for genetic manipulation and genetic imprint. The extraterrestrials are upgrading our genetic coding based on advanced sacred geometric principles. This is done through the use of pure copper, pure gold, and crystal. The whole world is transforming and the Aquarian Mission is aligning with sacred places. People are receiving the extraterrestrial language through the codons and the codes which Mother Earth sends through the grid lines that connect the sacred places, the frequencies. Every living and nonliving thing in existence on Earth was created by the extraterrestrial scientists who used sacred math for their work.

The Star Beings guide the Aquarian Mission to the grid lines of sacred places all over the planet, where we do our work. We assist with this upgrading of genetic coding. The tools and instruments we use for the Aquarian Mission are perfect, high-energy instruments made by Tibetan monks in accordance with the same sacred geometric principles used to create the universe and our cells. Crystals function as a transformer, amplifying the normal energy of the brain so that its energy is enhanced. The crystals are then incorporated into the two pure metals—copper and gold—which conduct this energy. A blue quartz from Siberia is set in a pristine field and is surrounded by turquoise, lapis, and diamond which, as magnets, form a force of living elements that may be used with pure intent. I use this tool to project thought.

The Earth needs joy and happiness in every heart. The extraterrestrials want the seeds of joy and happiness to be spread. The Lords of Light and Liberation perform miracles, but only they know when it is time for the new communities to gather up the pearls of rightness, the energies necessary for transformation. These new communities are a new way of life where everybody helps each other to be free, to be who they are, and to live together in love and peace. The extraterrestrials guide us to do the work—the mission has been assigned.

Professor Moi-RA Dove: The main focus of the Aquarian Mission is to help raise the level of consciousness in downtrodden

Previous page:
Prayers
      by Theresa Bakens

Left:
Jaguar Medicine
      by Desiree
      Fitzgibbon

Below:
Seven Apostles
of the Sun
      by Scott Murray

Opposite (top left):
Meditation
      by Theresa Bakens

Opposite (top right):
Free Spirit
      by Jingalu

Opposite (bottom):
Return of the Ghost
Dancers
      by Colleen Kelly

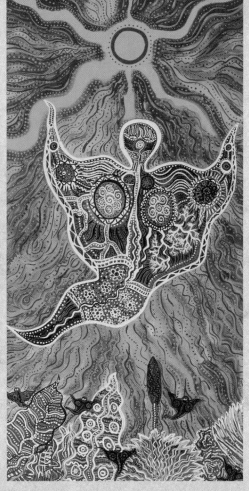

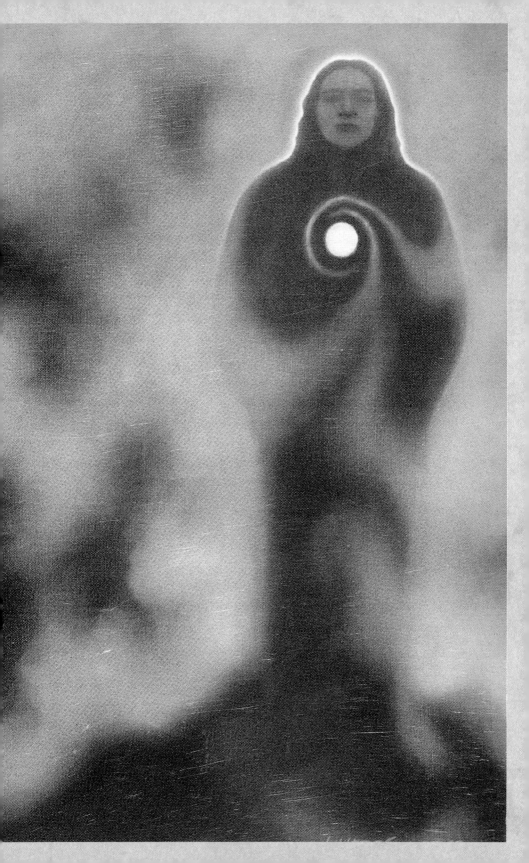

Opposite:
Brings the Sun
  by Catherine White-Swan

Above:
Ancestors
  by Jingalu

Below:
Holding the Universe Together
  by Jingalu

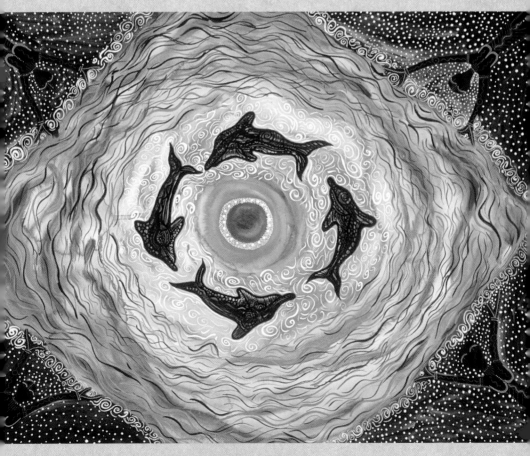

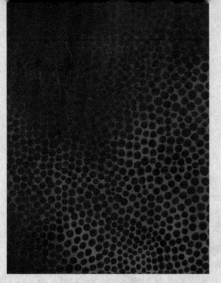

Opposite page (top):
Spirit Keepers of
the Four Directions
by Colleen Kelly

Opposite (bottom left):
Sunbow
by Scott Murray

Opposite (bottom right)
Dreamtime
by Theresa Bakens

Left:
Blood Ties
by Desiree Fitzgibbon

Below:
Dead Sea
by Mitch Gyson

Overleaf:
Feminine Crown
photograph by June

countries. We have different parts of the work. I teach love and compassion, and RA-Ja shares everything about truth and taking the dogma out of beliefs. We were sent first to the Philippines, because that is my native country. I'm sent to whatever place I need to be at a particular point in time. The first one was the Philippines. The second one was India and Nepal. The third and fourth were Israel and Palestine, to work on the path of peace. Next we are going to Mount Shasta.

My father is a famous philosopher. When I was a little girl, my father used to point me out to the visitors that came to see him and say, "This child of mine is an ancient soul, an old soul." When I grew up and undertook this mission, I realized the truth in what he was saying.

My soul came from Venus, the planet of love. Therefore, when I came down here, whatever is not love I do not understand. I permitted myself to be born on this planet. The Chohan of the Planetary Council said, "There's an emergency on this planet. How many of you would like to help?" I raised my hand and said, "I will." I permitted myself to be born in the Philippines because the 7,700 islands of the Philippines are the tips of the mountains of Lemuria. The energy of the Lemurians affects the people of the Philippines; that's why there are many healers there.

The Filipinos are a very loving people. Our ancestors were also very loving people. We were very late in experiencing modern life. There were no factories or technologies like we have now. When I was a child, if somebody needed to build a house, everybody came to help. They all contributed different materials. The women took care of the food and somebody played the guitar while the work got done. Nobody needed to spend money—they just got the best from the community. We brought the bamboo, and we offered everything that we had in the yard. In this way, there was no dependence on the economic system. It was beautiful. My mother had seven rice fields that she planted every year, and that is where most of our food came from. There were seven of us, and when we came in the barrio, the people there would say, "Come here, we have something to give you." And they'd give us a watermelon. When we got to the end of the barrio, every one of us had a watermelon in our hands. But now those places are not there anymore; a cement factory was built over it. The mountain nearby has the materials to make cement, so it was purchased. Cement factories emit so much smoke and dust that people can't grow anything anymore—the plants will not grow under such conditions. The men were taken on as workers in the factory. The women take care of the children. The cement dust killed everything. The houses are full of dust; it makes many people sick.

When I was growing up, I had spirit guides who always talked to me, and I talked to them. They would tell me what was going to happen in my life—every day they would tell me things. I didn't think this was unusual; I thought that everybody had spirit guides. My spirit guides often came in dreams. For instance, a dream that I had before I gave birth said I would have a baby girl, which I did. In another dream, I was taken out of this world to Hades, the land of the dead. I met an old woman there, and she said, "Come here, come here. I know who you are, and I want to show you the heart of your uncle." My uncle, Juan Ortega, is the founder of the Spiritualist movement in the Philippines. He was a leader in the community. I used to go the Center of the Spiritualists, even as a little child. I remember that on Good Friday my uncle would recite the seven last words of Jesus. I would listen very intently. In the services, a spirit guide gave a message for the whole group through a medium with a *parato*—a revolving table. The medium read the message, and the people talked about it. The last one to speak was my uncle, who was the director of the center. He talked about when the soul was in Venus, the planet, and I particularly listened to that. I did not know that my uncle got all his messages from the Theosophical Society. He borrowed all the books about Theosophy from the Philippines Library and was teaching Theosophy to the group of Spiritualists. When he died, my sister said, "Arrange the books of Uncle in the library." That was when I saw all the books he had on Theosophy. So I had been receiving the Theosophical teachings since I was five years old.

When I was in my first year in college, I majored in philosophy, and then I learned the Hindu teachings as well as those of Buddhism, and Christianity. My heart was close to Buddhism, since I had practiced it since I was a little child. Buddhism is a religion of compassion and love, and the Filipino nation is based on love and peace. I say this because I grew up in that environment of peace and love, which comes from the Lemurian energy.

I remember the teachings from Lemuria. In Lemuria there were tall crystals on both sides of the streets, and everybody received all the energy from those crystals. A very naughty child wasn't spanked or scolded. Instead, the Lemurians placed him or her on a chair under a small pyramid hung from the ceiling. They meditated and put crystals around the child. The crystals emitted positive energy and balanced the child's energy. At that time, they didn't have candies, sugars, and sweets making the child hyperactive, which is happening now. I feel that every extraterrestrial, every Star Being, is very intelligent and very knowledgeable. The extraterrestrials, beings from other planets, are working very closely with Lemurian energy.

The first course that we offer at the Aquarian Mission is called Star Soul Attunement. Star Soul Attunement is attuning the soul to the "star being-ness" of origin. We make a slit in the aura of people so that they can look out. Like a chrysalis, the aura opens up, and the butterfly soul comes out. Star Soul Attunement is a form of psychic surgery. This kind of surgery is done not on the physical body but on the etheric. This is not like other surgeries where they open up the wound and you see the blood coming out. I look at the etheric body and clean up things that are not supposed to be there. My way of healing is for the spirit—the spiritual healing of the soul. Psychic surgery healings have two parts. The first is a consultation in which I talk to the patient. The second part is spiritual. I take out the blockages—all the fears, vows, and unpleasant childhood events that the patient cannot let go of and cannot forgive. The main point of etheric surgery is forgiveness. Illness first comes from outside the body and then becomes a sickness of thinking and feeling. Only after that does the physical body experience illness because whatever is

Sign of the Dove

thought out in the etheric automatically happens in the physical. So the mental aberrations and emotional trauma a person has experienced register as illness in the physical. All ailments can be healed, however. As soon as I see the patient's face, when we meet for the first time, I can see everything I need to know by the way she moves, the way she walks, the way she talks, the way she carries her head. This is my "soul reading."

My main work on this planet is to spread peace and love and to let people know that we must take care of the feminine energy so that it may go up onto a higher level of consciousness. The masculine energy will honor and respect the feminine as it used to be—before the time when men would put us on a pedestal. That is precisely why I came here to this planet, to help in this transition.

The Divine World Mother—known as Quan Yin in China and by different names in different countries and cultures—is the Holy Mother. Quan Yin, whose name means "Hearer of the Cries of the World," is the Bodhisattva of Compassion. She is the most beloved of Chinese deities, and her mantra is *om-mani-padme hum,* "hail the

Sky Spirit

jewel or pearl in the lotus." Quan Yin is the patron saint for the women of fishing villages.

Many people are masters—masters of education, masters of philosophy, masters of technology, masters of art—but they don't know how to love. How can a master be a master if he or she is not a loving being? According to the teachings of Theosophy, you must pass through phases of development before you can become a master. It's like climbing a stairway; you must climb from step to step before you reach the top.

It is time now for peace to reign over the world; this is the prophecy we must put out in the world. We are all brothers, all one. We are at a crossroads. If we can get rid of our ties to religious affiliations and countries of origin, if we can stop saying, "I want to go back to where I came from, my country, my people, my religion. . ." and start thinking, "there's no more 'my-my-my,'" then everybody will welcome everybody. We'll say, "You're welcome here, come here." You can have an exodus in one part of the world, another exodus in a different part of the world—north, south, east, and west—

it will not matter. People will be free to travel as they like. There will be no more war because we will have no need to fight for territory or for religious beliefs or points of origin. Peace is going to start. Peace is starting now, and some people, putting positive thoughts ahead of time, even say that there is peace now. If everybody could believe this wholeheartedly, it would be reality. If we disseminate this concept to all, and we think on it and pray on it and believe in it, then peace is here. Because if you are negative, more negativity comes in. But if you are positive, all the possibilities that you make come in. Let's concentrate on all the good works. Let's ask "how can I be of service to others?" That is love. It says in the Bible, "Seek you first the Kingdom of Heaven." Do this and everything is the Creator's part. The Creator is omniscient, omnipotent, and omnipresent. Ask "How can I be of service" and everything will come to you. Every morning when I wake up, I say, "Be joyful every morning." When things are happening that are not positive, I just sing. When things appear to be falling down, the two of us say, "No, we're going on." When we are joyful we shine with light, and we become lighter and lift ourselves from the negative energy. As we become lighter and lighter, we reach that level of consciousness where we can get together with the masters and teachers who are already there. That is the Aquarian Perspectives Interplanetary Mission.

Star Soul Attunement

An   Aquarian Mission   Of   Merging Cultures

The Rainbow   Prophecy   Other Flesh

Other Tongues   Coming Together

Compassionate Enlightenment   In Joy   And   Peace

Attuning   The Soul   To Star   Being-ness

Of   Our Origin   A Butterfly   A Cocoon

The Chrysalis   Is Open   To Receive

Love   Wings Fly   On   The Healing   Process

A Soul   Reborn   From   Another Realm

Another Planet   Of the Stars

Sharing a Message   From   The Culture   Bearers

The Extraterrestrial Wisdom   Of All Times

Colors   Of   The Rainbow

Awaken   Our Memories   For Our Purpose

The Mission   Healing   Planet Earth

From   Falling   On   Us All

Aboriginal rock painting pictographs are the oldest surviving form of art found in many regions of the Australian territory. The date of the actual creation of these rock art galleries is still debated; there are widely contradictory views on the age of the ancient sacred sites at which they are found. It is generally agreed, however, that the oldest rock pictograph is well over thirty thousand years old. The indigenous people themselves, the Aborigines, believe that they have been in Australia since the beginning of time—the creation known as the Dreamtime. The Aboriginal time line stretches back one hundred thousand years. I have been told by Aborigines that before that there was nothing, but prior to that, there were beings not of this Earth, remnants of whom can still be found.

10 Painting in the Dreamtime

Holding the Universe

JINGALU
*Australian Bunjalung and
Birigan Gargle Yeagle Aborigine Artist*

*In the time of Alcheringa, the land lay flat and
cold. The world, she empty. The Rainbow Serpent,
she asleep under the ground with all the
animal tribes in her belly waiting to be born.
When it be time, she push up.*

OODGEROO, ABORIGINE NOONUCCAL POET

Jingalu

Jingalu is a member of the Bunjalung and Birigan Gargle Yeagle Aborigine tribes from the far north coast of New South Wales. Independent at the age of fifteen, she was accepted at the prestigious Fine Arts department of Cairnes College of Tafe for Aboriginals and Islanders. Jingalu embarked on a career that has combined painting and teaching in Aboriginal art, culture, and history. She has exhibited extensively in both Australia and North America. In 1996, she was the winner of the inaugural Indigenous Arts Fellowship. She has written and illustrated a book on the Dreamtime stories of her people.

My people are the Aborigines of Australia, and my heritage derives from two tribes: Birigan Gargle Yeagle and Bunjalung. Dolphins are the Yeagle tribe's totem. Dolphins hold symbolic meaning both as part of our mythology and as a sign of good luck. We are never allowed to kill a dolphin for food; instead, we protect and look after them. Like many tribes around the world, we believe that there is a spirit in everything—which is why there are totems for everything in the land. We believe in reincarnation. Our creation stories say that people have come from and turned into kangaroos, and kangaroos have turned into people. Birds and dolphins, too, have turned into people. We also believe in Spirit Trees.

Aboriginal creation stories tell us how the world and its laws came to be made. The stories of my paintings come from what I have been told as a child growing up. They are about the way the land was created over here in Australia. The Clarence River is a big river that I grew up near. As the story goes, a great sea serpent came up onto the land. With each step he took, he made a crevice that filled up with water. Then he became stuck, which created one of the islands. There are stories of how the stars came to be up near the moon because the Ancestors threw coals up in the air. Then there's Bawal, the Feather Foot Man. He is very powerful and can travel in any element of nature. He can heal people if they are not well or curse them if they have broken Aboriginal law. Bawal is the most powerful figure in my tribe. He is our law enforcer. He is our protector.

My childhood was very happy. I grew up on the north coast of New South Wales. I had a huge family. As I've gotten older, I've realized what a unique childhood I had. I lived with my mum, and my uncle and auntie—who had six or seven kids—as well as another uncle who was my auntie's brother and my Grandfather, who was my mum's father. All in all there were fifty-seven people living in our little three-bedroom house. We all lived together in that small house. That's what it's like in the Aboriginal community here—the large extended family all lives together under one roof. Even though I never had siblings of my own, I had all my cousins. According to Aboriginal Law and customs cousins are the same as sisters and brothers. In our tradition, like Native Americans, we have matriarchal family lines. In our custom, the mother-in-law is not allowed to talk to her daughter's husband, so there is no intermixing of things. There is no one word with which to group together all Aboriginal people, such as "clan." We are more like tribes, and our totems symbolize the area we live in. A lot of our stories are about male places and female places which are sacred and taboo to speak about. We teach the young ones to stay away from certain places. We also teach a general respect amongst the young ones and within the culture. Most of us Aborigines believe in our stories but other people here still laugh at our beliefs.

Although Australia has become much more multicultural than it used to be, there is still racism. Aborigines have many legal rights now, but people seem to think that we should all be under one nation, which negates the potential for indigenous sovereignty. There are organizations that are set up purely for protecting our rights. People find it hard to cope with the fact that we have a few so-called advantages over them. Even with many positive contemporary changes, we are still living through the prejudices that people learned during their childhoods. These prejudices have been carried into adulthood and we still have to cope with that.

Some time ago, I had an experience with the Fire and the Spirit Man up in an area called Laura. I was with an Aborigine friend from art school, Bonnie, and her son, William, on a campout. One night we decided to sleep out under the stars, by the fire. The fire was burning down as we got ready to go to sleep. No one had put it out because it was in the Bora Ring, a huge circle in which the men have their ceremonies. The Bora Ring is a dancing place for "Men's Business" and "Women's Business"—the initiations and rites of passage for men and women—so it is sacred and not to be entered. I was closest to the fire, and I was looking at it when all of a sudden I saw a figure sitting there, crouching down. I motioned to

Bonnie to have a look, but she was half asleep and told me to go to sleep, too. I looked over at the fire and I still saw him. He was a traditional man, dressed in the old way, semi-naked. He had the traditional hair, which is dreadlocks. In the Aboriginal tradition, the higher dreadlocks are worn on the head, the more prominent the person is within the tribe. The dreads were very high on this man's head. I watched him for a while before he disappeared. No one spoke about the vision until we got back to Cairnes, where we lived. About three days later, I asked Bonnie what she had seen, and she said that she saw the fire turning to coals and the man disappearing. I decided to talk to my uncle about it, and he told me that I was nearly "sung," or had my spirit taken—sometimes people say, "He'll sing ya" or "You'll be sung." My uncle told me that is what the Spirit Man was trying to do to me. He said a lot of old men used to do that to young women or people who they otherwise would not be able to catch. They take your spirit. Spirit Man takes you and

SACRED NIGHTS
by Jingalu

your spirit leaves your body. I was the youngest woman. There was another older woman, in her sixties, who said she heard singing and women's voices trying to talk to her.

What we call the "song lines" is the interconnectivity of all things. They are grid lines that connect along Earth and then go into the Universe. The song lines connect to places that are most full of energy—energy points. In Australia there is a song line at La Rue which goes out to the Blue Mountains. I have heard different stories over the years about how the song lines are connected to the Star People. We believe that we are always on the journey with the song lines.

There has been a lot of UFO activity in Australia, especially up in the Northern Territory, which is very isolated. There are still a lot of traditional Aboriginal people up there, living in the same ways as they did in the past, having rituals and living off the land. Whether or not they are associating with the extraterrestrials, I don't know for sure. But there are always a lot of sightings up there that are written up in the newspapers. There are also a lot of Armed Forces up that way. When there's a sighting, they go out and try to verify whether it was a routine flight. If it wasn't, they announce that it was an unidentified flying object.

I definitely believe that there are other races of beings from other worlds. Otherworldly events have been seen and well documented in the Aboriginal communities. Certain people will talk about it. My uncle, who has passed on, used to see UFOs quite regularly. He was careful with who he talked to about such things, and mostly he kept his experiences to himself. A lot of the older Aboriginal people have also seen these things and, like my uncle, only talk about them with certain people.

There are caves here, called rock art galleries, that are filled with ancient Aboriginal pictographs, like the ancient Hopi and Navajo drawings you can find in the southwestern United States. All the indigenous peoples have drawings like these; they are a way of telling stories, keeping history, and passing on messages. The rock art paintings here in Australia are unusual. The paintings on the cave walls express how Aborigines have survived since the beginning of time—since our people came here. Some of them depict beings that don't look exactly human, and others show what look like spacecraft or flying saucers. Archaeologists have undertaken digs up near the rock art galleries. They can trace our people back only so far, and then they encounter a period where no one seemed to be living here. But they have found remnants of beings that they can't explain from a time period even before that. They aren't of this earth; they aren't human. I reckon the Aborigines come from Sirius. I don't remember if this is something that I have been told or something that I've formulated from my own perception; I've heard that there is a direct line for us Aborigines to Sirius. This has come to me over a period of years, from people in the family—from my Grandfather and my uncles.

One of my first paintings is called *Earth Forest,* and it represents the land I come from and the elements of everything—the earth, the sea, the sky, the sun, and our spirit—tied together. There are lot of little frogs in the painting. The day we don't see any frogs, we will be near the end of our time on Earth. When I was young, I always saw green tree frogs. If you went outside to the loo and lifted up the seat, there was always a frog or a red-back spider that had crawled underneath. But then, for a long time, there weren't any frogs, anywhere. So when I started painting, at the age of fifteen, I always put the frogs in the canvas. I would have a little frog in every piece, sort of like a signature. Like us, the frogs need the water to survive. My painting *Night Swimming* shows humans starting their life as creatures of the sea before adapting to the land, similar to the frogs. Drawing from my dreams, I believe that every living thing started in water. This is also what science tells us. As a coastal person, this has had a big influence in my life. In the beginning, we crawled along the earth from the sea and then rose up as humans.

Now the women are holding up the world, holding the universe together. Even though people may lose their way, the customs will always find a path for them. My grandparents' hope lies in the survival of our culture. The Elders have been through so much to have survived to this point. They are distraught about the state of the planet, but what they are even more distraught about are the young ones. Here and throughout the world, the young ones have so much depression. Among the Aboriginal people, and even in my own family, depression has led to suicides, mostly by young men. I have cousins who drowned themselves and others who hanged themselves. The Elders are most concerned about these young ones. It comes back to culture: The Elders think that the youth have no culture now and that is why they are dying. They have no direction and no self-esteem about who they are and where they are from. The Elders see that hope can be found within keeping the tradition of the culture alive. The answer lies within one's own family, supporting and showing love to each other. That is where the hope is. When there aren't any gatherings and the stories don't get passed along, the culture starts to get lost. Keeping the Aboriginal family strong is a big concern for our future.

We need to get back to listening. The only thing that continues inside of us is spirit. So keep the spirit.

Holding the Universe

Women   Holding   The Universe   Together
The Young Ones   Holding   The Family
Even When   People   May Lose
Their Way   Traditions   Will   Find Them

Earth   Forest   The Sea   Dolphins
And Whales   The Totem   The Sun   Moon
And Stars   In Spirit   The Ancestors
Of Everything   The Ever Continuing
Circle   Of Life   All Forms

The Rock Art   Caves   Of Ancient Ones
Song Lines   Of Journeys   The Pathway
In Dreamtime   Painting   Sacred Nights
A Dance   An Honoring   To Life

Keeping   The Culture   Alive
Keeping   The Spirit
In Colors   And   Frequency   The Heartbeat
Of   The People

If we are to reach the threshold of a thousand years of peace, then we must be able to recognize the Great Spirit, the High God, the emanation of a Supreme Being, in every one of us. For if we cannot accept each other, then how can we accept life in forms from outside the universe? When the present cycle ends in 2012, contact with races of higher intelligence and consciousness will help usher in a new world and an era of peace—but only if we allow it to happen.

According to the Koran—the book of scripture revealed to the Prophet Muhammad in the seventh century—the first house of worship established on Earth was a simple stone structure located in the city of Mecca, in Saudi Arabia. There are passages in the Koran which describe life on Earth and life elsewhere. It refers to a time and place when contact will occur between extraterrestrials and humanity. It is not written, however, when this contact will take place.

11

A Gathering of Nations

Serving Mankind

Historian of Islam in Africa and the Americas

The ink of a scholar is more precious than the blood of a martyr.

MUHAMMAD, THE HOLY PROPHET

SULTAN ABDUL LATIF

Sultan Abdul Latif is of African American and Native American descent. He is also a scholar of the prophecies and records kept by many cultures. The author of two recent books, Slavery: The African American Psychic Trauma *and the recently released* When Nations Gather, *he lectures and speaks at many universities and religious organizations. He is the president of Latif Communications Group, Inc., a multimedia firm specializing in book publishing, newspaper publishing, and video and film productions. He is also the director of* The Media Connection, *a weekly television show featuring a variety of journalists and news that impacts the African American community. Mr. Latif serves as an educational consultant and media specialist for the Chicago Board of Education. A nationally renowned historian and teacher, he lives by the power of example and by the grace of Allah.*

Sultan means leader, chief, or ruler. I look upon this as a leader who should serve mankind independent of selfish reasons. *Abdul* means "servant of" and *Latif* is "an attribute of the Creator." The Creator is the most kind God; Sultan is therefore a spiritual position. I was not born with this name; I received it upon conversion to Islam. Like many African Americans with a Native American background, I was born and raised in the black ghetto. I was born in the 1940s. While I was growing up we were still called colored people. My cultural background is so varied and as I began to develop I found that there were a lot of historical and cultural inconsistencies. When I first heard of Islam, I was very attracted to it. I began to study it.

I accepted the religion of Islam because I believe it is the truth from God. Islam actually began in the 7th Century, in Arabia, when the Koran was revealed to the Prophet Muhammad. In the Holy Koran it says, "this day we have perfected your religion." God was speaking directly to mankind and this became known as Islam. According to Western historians, Muhammad was considered an ignorant man, but I prefer to use the word "unlettered." Ignorance is determined by one's actions, not by one's exposure to academic achievement. Muhammad was a successful merchant who was always known to be truthful and forthright. He had a wonderful respect for nature and human life, and he always protected the poor and the disenfranchised. He was known to spend time meditating in caves. One day while he was in a cave, the angel Gabriel appeared. Gabriel identified himself to Muhammad and told him to read the Koran. Muhammad said, "I cannot read." Gabriel told him that he could. Again, Muhammad said that he could not read. Finally Gabriel said, "Read in the name of your Lord." Then Muhammad began to recite the first chapter of what is called the Koran, the Holy Book or Sacred Book of Muslims. Some of the knowledge of extra-terrestrials and life on other planets was revealed at that time, through the Koran, to a man who was unlettered and unable to read. The Koran says that this book is for those who want to be rightly guided and that if you can produce something that is superior, then do so. Nobody has been able to produce anything more superior than the word of the Great Creator.

African Americans, in particular, can relate to Islam and the Koran because of a genetic memory. African Americans have a two-fold experience: first they hear the word of God and then they are influenced by it. This type of spiritual experience is available to all of mankind. The generosity of the Creator applies to everyone. This is because as human beings we are no different from one another. We are like our Native brothers and sisters who hear the call of the Great Spirit. Take, for example, the Hopi people and their pursuit of the spirit being Massau. The Hopi knew that Massau was on Earth, and they sought him out. When they saw him, his appearance was so frightening that some of the people ran. The ones who remained had been looking for him for such a long time, and they wanted to know what it was that Massau knew— What was his "Law"? They refused to leave, even though he had presented himself in such a horrifying manner. They were determined to receive the spiritual wisdom brought by Massau—no matter what. The moment that the people accepted Massau's physical appearance, his attitude began to change. He gave them wonderful knowledge that told them how to live and allowed their people to flourish. A wonderful example of humanitarianism, the Hopi became scholars and keepers of the sacred knowledge. Similarly, when Muslims whose hearts understand hear information coming from the Holy Koran, we have the same reaction as the Hopi did to Massau: Our hearts are lifted up, and our understanding of the Creator and mankind is changed.

The Hopi Prophecy and the religion of Islam are in harmony. The Hopi Prophecy concerning the second coming of the Massau, or the Messiah, is also discussed in the Koran. I write about this parallel between the Hopi Prophecy and the Koran in my book *When Nations Gather*. While I was working on this manuscript, a great chief came to me in my dreams and said, "Why did they criticize us for our songs and our prayers? They wanted to cut us off because the rhythm that we use put us in touch with the Creator. This rhythm was given to us. They would criticize us, but if you go and search this out, you will find that our prayers are truthful!" In this dream I saw great chiefs riding on horses in what I understood to be the Trail of Tears. They appeared much larger then what they would have been in reality. They were elaborately dressed in garments and feathers. It seemed that they went on for miles and miles, there were so many of them. I could hear the rhythm of drums and them singing their songs. The head chief at the front said to me, "I represent all the great chiefs. When we sing our songs and dance, this is how we give thanks to the Creator. When our White Brothers came they did not understand. They attacked us and called us uncivilized. But their great prophet, Solomon, wrote the Song of Songs. Didn't they understand that our songs were sung for the Great Creator? So who is the savage—the one who oppresses or the one who sings the songs to the Creator?"

I woke up and thought, "my God, the Song of Solomon!" I went to the book—to the actual Song of Solomon. In English, it is the "Song of Solomon" but in Hebrew it is the "Song of Songs," Sheer Ha Sheer-Reem. There is something totally inconsistent when, in the Western religion, a Prophet of God can be in the part of the Bible called the Song of Solomon but, simultaneously, the songs of native people are destroyed and disrespected. The prophecies—such as those from the Hopi tradition—said that the White Brother had forgotten the Divine Law and there would be total chaos. This principle has been manifested. Now the songs, dances, and prayers have returned.

As an African American with a Native American background I walk two paths in my mission; my quest for the Divine compelled me to respect both paths and realize that they lead to the same place. There are many records of cultural interaction between Africans and Native Americans prior to the European colonization of the American continent. Historian Ivan Van Sertama has researched and documented extensively both the arrival of African people on this continent and the traveling of Native American peoples around the world. It is a tremendous history. I interviewed a Native American sister from Old Mexico who told me that her people had records of the West African emperor Abubakari landing there. There were also many Spanish explorers, including Balboa, who talked about encounters with Native Americans voyaging to Africa. If you look at the Cherokee language, and the work of Sequoya, you can see Arabic as the basis for interpreting the Cherokee alphabet. The words of the Cherokee are parallel to those of the Arabic language. There had to have been contact between these peoples.

I spoke with a Pipe Carrier from the Ottawa Nation in Canada who told me that his people had interacted with African people long before the arrival of Europeans. The artwork, symbols, and color systems of the two cultures are similar. A few years ago an African shaman went to the Ottawa to meet one of their shamans, who they call Medicine People. He wanted to speak to the Ottawa about the similarities between their cultures and in certain ritual practices. He came to find out what the Ottawa had retained from the sacred knowledge. The two men were sitting together at a table drinking Coca-Cola when one of the cans moved from a spot in front of the Ottawa Medicine Person across the table to a spot in front of the African shaman. Then the African shaman moved it back to the Ottawa Medicine Person. Neither of the two men was touching the can, but it kept moving back and forth between them. Finally the Ottawa man asked if the African shaman had come all this way to test him. The African said no. He said that he had come to reunite with his brothers.

Native peoples all over the world have been disfranchised, culturally oppressed, and subjected to genocide and serious crimes against humanity because of the arrival of Europeans into their

AFRICAN SHAMAN
by Dorit Bat Shalom

land. This gives me a great sadness. So much wonderful knowledge of indigenous peoples has been completely destroyed. In the Mayan culture alone, fourteen thousand books on stone and bark tablets were destroyed by the Spanish. I express this sadness in my prayers. One night I was sitting in my bedroom, praying. I began to hear what sounded like stampeding. Then I saw a herd of maybe a thousand buffalo charging at me. At first I thought I should run, but then I thought, "Wait, I'm in my room—this must be an illusion." Then the Buffalo communicated to me and said, "Don't listen with your ears. Listen with your heart. We lived for thousands of years with our Native Brothers. We were willing to supply all their needs including food, clothes, tools, and many instruments for their survival. We were happy with our arrangement with our Native Brothers and we had grown to be a hundred million strong. See, the Natives ate our meat, but when they died they would return to Earth and there would be beautiful green grass that would grow, and we would eat that grass. We were all part of the circle of life. But when our White Brothers came, we could not understand how they could just kill us thousands and thousands at a time. We thought that these people must be really hungry. But then we realized they just wanted us for our skins as trophies. They would call us dumb animals because we wouldn't run from them. But the Great Creator created us and he gave man dominion over Earth to act responsibly and take only what they need. And if we had sought to hide, they would have only pursued to kill us. So I ask them this question: Who was the dumb animal—the one who acts according to the natural order of things or the one who kills one hundred million of us? Little did they know that when they killed our Indian Brothers and us they were killing themselves—and loosing their souls. So go, and tell my story. Go and tell the story of the buffalo. And we know you will tell our story truthfully, because the Indian Brother called you all the people of the buffalo."

If someone asked me why I was on my mission, I would say, "unconditional love." Unconditional love means that if you see things that are incorrect, you voice your opinion, even if it means death. This is why I struggle and fight to say what happened to Leonard Peltier was incorrect; I say that Nelson Mandela never gave up his spirit during his long incarceration and hold him up as an example of what we can do to struggle against what is wrong. I speak about the incarceration of journalist Mumia Abu Jamal, because he fights the war of the pen, and that is what the government is afraid of—not the war of the gun, the war of the pen. It is essential for us to realize that we are in battle for life itself. The strongest armament, the strongest instrument that we have, is the pen. The New World Order has taken everything from us. All we have left is our spirit, our dreams, and our pens.

The Koran discusses the coming together of various life forms in the universe. In chapter 42, called Al-Shura, it states in part, "Among his [the Creator's] signs is the Creation of the Heavens, and the Earth, and whatever living creatures he has spread forth in both." It doesn't say that the Creator spread forth only creatures of Earth. It says that in the heavens—as well as on Earth—there are living beings. This means that all living forms follow the Great Creator Spirit. So when beings from the heavens come to Earth, they are coming with the permission of the Creator to verify that all the prophets—those of the Hopi, Crazy Horse, Muhammad, Buddha, and others—will be justified. This was written fourteen hundred years ago, in a cave, by a man who could not read or write.

Ancient indigenous people could have encountered extraterrestrials. A spacecraft was documented to have landed and crashed in Tibet some twelve thousand years ago. The extraterrestrials were described by the Tibetan people as having large heads and very small bodies. In 1938, in caves in the mountains of Baya Kara-Ula, on the border between China and Tibet, archaeologists found graves containing skeletons of beings with small bodies and large, overdeveloped heads. In those same caves, on the walls, archaeologists found petroglyphs of the rising sun, the moon, unidentifiable stars, and the earth all joined together by lines of pea-size dots. The cave drawings are thought to be some twelve thousand years old.

Along with the skeletons, the archaeologists found a large round

CAVE DRAWING PETROGLYPH, SAHARA

stone disk. It had a hole in its center and was carved with a long spiral groove of written letters. When the disks were tested in Russia, they were found to contain large quantities of cobalt and other metals. The disks vibrated, emitting a rhythm similar to an electric charge. This charge passed through all discs, as if they were an electrical circuit board. No one could translate its meaning until 1985, when Dr. Tsum Umi Nui of China broke the code and started to unravel the "talking" grooves. In 1965, more stone disks were found in the same caves—716 of them. They told the story of a mission by the inhabitants of another planet who came to the Baya Kara-Ula mountain range. These alien beings called themselves the Dropas. They had crashed and had no way to build another spaceship, and so they stayed. Many of them had been hunted and killed by the Han tribe, who lived in other caves. Legends of that area speak of small yellow-faced men who came from the clouds long ago. The men had huge heads and tiny bodies. They were, in fact, considered ugly, which is why they were killed. These descriptions fit the bodies found in the caves. These caves are still inhabited by two semi-troglodyte types known as the tribes of the Hans and the Dropas. They are neither Chinese nor Tibetan, and they are barely five feet tall and are rather frail-looking.

This story of alien beings making their home on Earth is really fascinating, but it is not isolated. Each race has a tablet or sacred writing that refers to the period humanity is currently experiencing. The Dogon people of West Africa, for example, claim to have descended from the people of the star Sirius. The Dogon have a prophecy that says that they will return to Sirius one day—that they will be taken back to Sirius and they are waiting for certain events to take place. Whenever the planet Sirius comes into orbit of the solar system, the Dogon have a great celebration. The Dogon have tried to explain this prophecy to people. The Dogon claim that they were originally in North Africa, inhabiting Egypt. Then they migrated farther into the interior because they had to protect the sacred knowledge. They say that they taught many of the ancient prophets, and they still retain certain practices and healing skills that are not of Earth. When European scientists studied the Dogon, they were amazed by the knowledge they possessed.

I believe that extraterrestrials are going to have some influence on our future. Mother Earth is reclaiming herself, and there is a purification going on. In testaments written by many prophets, these things were predicted. I think it is essential now for us to understand what the elders of all nations are saying: that we must respect the sacred knowledge and come together to compare the parts of the puzzle. If we can do only one thing, it should be to agree that we all have a similar desire to protect Mother Earth, the environment, and all people. Then, if the extraterrestrials do arrive, we will be prepared. We should not rely on them coming back to make the changes we need to survive. They are not coming to save the human race; we have to do that. It's our responsibility.

If the extraterrestrials come back, it will be only to verify that our people are on the right path by being in harmony with the natural law and becoming people that are divine. Contact will verify that the Great Creator of all of us has protected us—even in our demise. The extraterrestrials return as a perfect example to not only the people of Earth but the whole solar system and the whole universe so that we will no longer think in terms of just being linear. We will begin to think in terms of being interdimensional. The

RIBBON OF THE EXPANDING UNIVERSE
by Tula

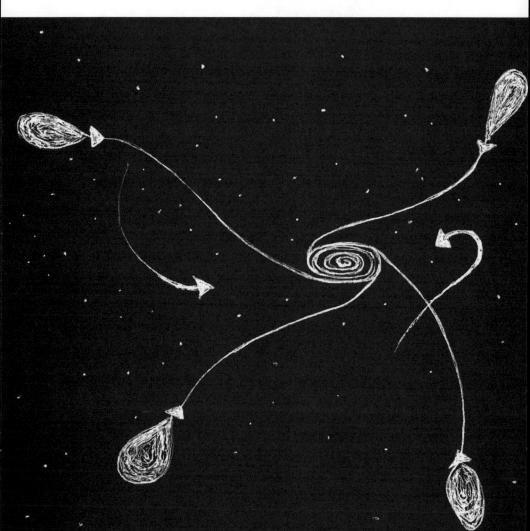

extraterrestrials may also have the technology to help us reclaim Earth.

The Koran speaks of seven planetary heavens, each one consisting of seven planets. This would mean that there are a lot of different forms in the universe. In the Koran (translation under the auspices of Hadrat Mirza Nasir Ahmed) verse 21:05 it says, "As we begin the first creation so shall we repeat it, a promise binding on us that we shall certainly fulfill."

In *Revelations, Rationale, Knowledge, and Truth* by Mirza Tahir Ahmad this passage is elaborated upon:

> It has been clearly demonstrated that the entire universe would be drawn back into a black hole which later on would explode into another Big Bang—releasing its entrapped mass once again. From this the reader maybe misled to believe that the universe thus appearing and disappearing periodically will go on and on forever. The image on this page presents the scientific vision of how the ultimate black hole may have devoured whatever was left of the universe, excretions from all around. As it approaches the horizon it is compressed into a ribbon-like form which, before seeking into the pit, revolves around it, because the pit itself is revolving. This resurrects in one's mind the image of a scribe rolling his scroll as mentioned in the verse 21:105 of the Koran: 'Remember the day when we shall roll up the heavens like the rolling up of scrolls.'

In the chapter of the Koran called Al-Shura it is written: "And He has the power to gather them together Jam-i-him, when He so please." The word *Jam-i-him* can mean contact either physically or through communication. Only the future will tell when this contact will occur, although it was predicted more than fourteen hundred years ago. The day will come when the scientists and the archaeologists will begin to unravel these mysteries, and when this happens you will know that the time is close. The time is close at hand, but it is essential for people to believe in the Great Creator of all things. The future will be granted to us based upon the fact that we will be providing the knowledge of these mysteries to our people, so that their hearts will change. They will become better people. You don't have to worry about the violence or think that because of some national situation we need to use guns. That is for the people with the fire—the Keepers of the Fire who build weapons of mass destruction. They are called Majol and Rajol in the Koran and Gog and Magog in the Bible. They need to realize that they have taken the wrong path in respect to the use of fire. None of the Creator's guardianships may be misused. The prophecies of old warned about this misuse. The Koran says that the European Christian nations would loose touch with the Creator in the latter days. They have historically manifested the end-time evil that was foretold in various traditions—not by any inherent nature, but through their chosen actions. The Creator's plan is for all of us to come together in harmony, to turn back to the Great Spirit, or whatever you call that All-Powerful Being. Turn towards "Him" and send your prayers. That is the most powerful weapon we have.

It is written that the day will come to pass when we understand that there is life on other planets. The future lies in our hands. We must realize that we ourselves are divine. Go back, explore all the sacred knowledge, the sacred writings—make it available to your people. We must realize that we are all one human family. We must come together and respect each other and respect Earth, for the Great Creator of all of us is watching.

Assalam Alaikum wa Rahmatullah

May Peace be upon you and the blessing of Allah.

Serving Mankind

To Serve   Mankind   For   The Greatest Good

Is   The Highest Work   We Can Perform

In Learning   To   Truly Accept   Each Other

As Brothers   And Sisters   Of   The Creator

For We   The Human   Family   Hold

The Responsibility   For   Each Color   Each Race

To Determine   Our Destiny   And Interaction

With   The Elder Species   The Extraterrestrials

Lift Up   Your Heart   To   The High God

And Goddess   Of All Beings

In All Realms   The Ancestor Spirits

Are Watching   Us   As We Gather   The Nations

Together   A Time   And   A Place

Where   Contact   Will Occur

A   First House   Of   Worship

The   Word   A Blessing   A Sacred Writing

The Most Powerful   Weapon   To Serve   Mankind

Now is a time of great change and preparation. We can choose which path to take as the way unfolds before us. We can be as Prophecy Rock at Orabi in Hopiland indicates: "a two-heart or a one-heart." A two-heart follows the path of power and greed, which is the road of ultimate destruction. The one-heart stays on the spiritual path of service to humanity and abides by the principle of working toward the greater good. We are all faced with the choice of which way to go. We are faced with the tasks of planting seeds and nurturing and cultivating our food source—Earth. As we step forward, we have all the teachings to hold; our hands are full of promise. We can exercise this promise as a fulfillment of prophecy, as the world cycles transform us.

12

Sunbow

World Cycles

NAOKO HITOMI
Japanese Healer

This world will be destroyed; also the mighty ocean will dry up; and this broad earth will be burnt up. Therefore, sirs, cultivate friendliness; cultivate compassion.

BUDDHIST TEACHING
FROM THE *VISUDDHI-MAGGA*

NAOKO HITOMI

Naoko Hitomi was born in Tokyo, Japan, in 1947. She is a board member and cofounder of Sunbow Five Foundation for Planetary Healing, which uses three principles—Johrei, nature cultivation, and art—to heal the individual. She is a past president of International Environmental Associates LTP, a Boston-based company that cleans up sites of environmental pollution, and also a past president of Cultural Exchange Associates, an educational exchange program, of Boston and Tokyo. Naoko is the mother of three and a beautiful spirit.

The sunbow is the rainbow circle around the sun. At the time of Noah's ark, the Creator had given humanity half of the half. Now he has given us a complete circle rainbow. This is the Creator's promise of healing: a complete circle. We named our foundation Sunbow Five because it is a phrase I have heard in my prayers and intuition. Five can represent the five different continents, the five colors, and the five root races. The Natives say that there are four races, but I have been to Hawaii, where the Hispanic people consider themselves to be not black, white, or red, but brown.

The first principle of the Sunbow Five Foundation is *Johrei*. The founder of this Johrei is Meishu-sama. One day, a long time ago, he channeled knowledge from the Creator which informed that the spirit world has turned from darkness into light. Whatever happens in the physical world is first manifested in the spiritual world. The spirit world has recently changed from darkness into light and the physical world in which we are living now will be greatly affected. Johrei focuses on this time of purification, when darkness in the spirit world has turned to light. Jesus Christ called this time the Last Judgment; Buddhism speaks of this time as being difficult for humanity; Native American prophecy calls it the time of purification. Meishu-sama has explained that this is happening because of all the negative karma that humanity has created.

As part of the purification, the energy of fire will increasingly enter this planet and everything will begin to melt. We can see evidence of this in global warming. The energy of fire will also start melting everything inside of us, that is, our spiritual selves. Everything we could have hidden before we cannot hide anymore. When you have a lot of light you can see everything. Even if we want to hide our feelings we will no longer be able to do so. We are entering into an age of crystal clear time.

Because of the intensity of fire in nature, people start to panic during the purification process. During this time many people die very fast—many people suffer. Western medicine is not sufficient to stop this. The Sunbow Five Foundation is trying to help people understand this purification process so we will suffer less. We teach how to cleanse the self prior to the physical manifestation of this purification. We can help people when people start to go through difficult times.

Sunbow Five works to create a happy, healthy home using Johrei, which means purifying the spirit with the energy of fire to release all karmic, physical, and spiritual toxins. When we are born, we already have the physical toxins of our ancestors as well as their spiritual karma. Johrei practitioners, using the energy of fire, use their hands to heal without actually touching people. This purifies the spiritual body. All the chemicals that we consume—through Western medicines, recreational drugs, or even agricultural products—are in our body. Everything that we have taken into our body which has not been flushed out creates illness. There is a chemical reaction the body has to all the intake of other chemicals. This happens when we eat foods with color additives or when we eat foods with chemical preservatives and pesticides. When people say, "I have a headache," they take medicine or drugs which still stay in the body. This chemical reaction affects the nervous system, creating sickness and disease. Johrei focuses on cleansing and purifying ourselves and melting away the toxins.

Many people come to our foundation with a serious disease such as cancer or multiple sclerosis. Frequent Johrei sessions, over time, can begin to melt the mucous or chemicals staying in the body. Johrei melts the toxins and then they pass out of the body. For instance, what is appendicitis? It is the area, on the right-hand side of the body, where toxins gather because the kidneys are not functioning well. At a certain point, the kidneys are not able to do the work of flushing the toxins from the body. When this happens, the toxins accumulate and gather in the appendix area, which causes appendicitis. We give energy into the kidneys then people get black, black diarrhea which means toxins are being released. With Johrei, people get cured. Not everybody, however, is healed;

Sunbow

because of the way we think and the way we lead our lives, some people choose not to forgive. Johrei is not a human power, it is the Creator's power and energy.

The second principle of Sunbow Five is nature cultivation. Nature cultivation is a farming method that does not use any chemicals—not even compost or manure. Instead, we garden with just three elements: the sun, the moon, and the soil. Together, these three elements create completely natural and healthy vegetables.

People have forgotten the power of soil. When the soil is alive, it has all the power to create the food we need. When we put pesticides, herbicides, and fertilizers into the soil, it is like us taking too much medicine; the soil loses its power. Now we see all these huge farms with their soil flying. When the soil doesn't have energy, it doesn't stay together—it flies. This is called erosion, and it's happening on major farms all across the world. But when the soil is alive, it sticks together. Soil is made slowly, by decaying matter: insects, earthworms, and more. The very top layer, called topsoil, is the most fertile, and also the most fragile. It takes nature one hundred years to create topsoil that is one centimeter deep. When we started one farm project they had about twenty-five centimeters of topsoil. This is about eight inches, which means that it took nature 2,500 years for that topsoil to be created. Underneath the topsoil is subsoil, which is lighter in color. This eventually turns into topsoil. In nature cultivation, we use only the topsoil, and we reuse it and feed it.

We consider soil precious, since it has the power to create anything. We don't damage it with chemicals or even bad words. We pray every morning that all will be good for the community. We don't sing songs or do ceremonies or prayers as Native Americans do at the planting field. Yet when we plant the seeds, we do so in harmony with nature. When the first frost comes, Earth is said to breathe in, and that is when we end our growing season. The soil is allowed to rest and become purified through frost, rain, snow, and sunshine. Earth starts to breathe out on February 4th, and that is when our growing season begins again. We also plant in harmony with the spirits and the ancestors of the area. We don't do any crop rotation; we always grow the same vegetables in the same place. We don't need to rotate because we have live soil and live water. Water is the blood of Earth and so any contamination of the water is going to stop our survival on this planet.

We hope to create completely natural, healthy vegetables which create a healthy body. Our body is the element of soil combined with the blood—the water—running through it. We receive everything from the soil, Mother Earth, and when we die we turn into soil. If our body is made out of truly healthy food then when we die we can be part of the healthy soil. We do Johrei to many people every day, and our energy from that practice also goes into the soil. When I watch the Japanese farmers planting seeds, I can feel this energy of Johrei when they hold the seeds.

When we do nature cultivation, we do everything in accordance with nature. Then the vegetables are very strong against the natural climatic changes like hurricanes or drought. Two years ago we had a drought during the summer. Many farmers in the area lost a lot of vegetables. In comparison, we only had to water our fields once through that summer. Our method of cultivation—using just that small layer of topsoil to grow in—encourages our plants to grow very long and healthy roots. As opposed to chemically oriented farms, our roots grow very long and spread into different dimensions. Last year we had a hurricane, and all the fields were under water. Many farmers lost their produce, which rotted after it sank under the water. But after the water drained off the vegetables in our fields, they continued to grow.

The third principle or teaching of Sunbow Five is *gagaku,* which is a very traditional court music. Any art that promotes peace may satisfy this third principle—painting, singing, dancing, flower arranging, or even the tea ceremony—any form of art which creates peace and harmony will do.

SPIRITUAL BEINGS

Through our work at Sunbow Five, we can see that when we go along with nature, we and the world are strong. In our fields, when the frequencies are good, we can create vegetables that are good. Everything is a frequency of energy. To some extent we can use Johrei to affect that energy. But these frequencies and energies can affect more than fields. We don't want people to think Johrei creates all miraculous stories, because what we are doing, day after day, is ordinary grounding work. But there are lots of miracle stories. When the atomic bomb was dropped on Hiroshima and Nagasaki, there were people doing Johrei. When the energy has a high vibration, it can neutralize the effects of such events. These people, even if they were in locations where most people died, didn't themselves suffer from the effects of radiation. This is when prayer and the knowledge of exactly what is happening to this planet during purification benefits humanity.

We are focusing on helping people understand what purification in the human body is all about. The human body is a small cosmos, and experiences the same thing that is happening with the planet. We explain to people that when we cleanse and purify ourselves, as individuals, our energy manifests as cleansing and purifying for the bigger community, the country, and the planet.

I have been interested in other dimensions and different phenomena—including UFOs—since I was a child. I used to see into different dimensions. I would see incredible sunbows or rainbows. These were those beautiful things that people could see together on special days. Some of these special phenomena I have seen in Japan. My friends and neighbors and I saw this sight many times in Tokyo. The sunbows or rainbows gave me messages. The color around the sun would change and it would look less brilliant than normal. It would look as though it had a lid on it—no more bright than the moon—and I could see it really well. It was as if the sun had turned into a moon. Suddenly it would start circling and dancing, and I would see a second sun come out from behind it. The second sun would also dance, a sun dance. Then suddenly the colors would come; the sun would turn pink and then green. It would give a flash toward me, and then I would see UFOs dancing around.

Many years ago, Fatima and Mother Mary revealed themselves to children in Portugal. This miracle became known throughout the world. They gave messages—a prophecy—to the children, but the Pope and the Vatican are keeping the Fatima Prophecy secret. Just as Fatima and Mother Mary offered their prophecy, the sun danced in Japan. I called Junichi Yaoi—a very well-known director of most of the programs on UFOs and mysteries—to tell him he should see this phenomenon; it was incredible. It was during this vision that I began to understand what the purification meant.

The strongest message I received happened around the moon. One night, at about three in the morning, I heard a voice telling me to go outside. I did not want to go by myself, so I asked my husband to come out with me to see what was happening. It was a clear night with no clouds and a full moon. Around the moon was a complete circle rainbow, not the reddish circle that usually appears around the moon, but a complete sunbow. Then, suddenly, I saw a Mothership fly along that rainbow, around the moon. The ship was the shape of a cigar. I heard a voice say, "The joint work of space brothers and space sisters had begun," which meant that the joint work between human beings and space people had begun. When I see the different dimensions related to the rainbow, then I am guided toward certain things that I need to do. Usually I am guided to introduce certain people to each other. It took me a month and a half before the instructions related to this message came to me. I was washing my child's cloth diapers when I finally understood the meaning behind this message.

Individual people from different countries have certain missions with regard to Star People. Japan is a country of the Spirit, so we have a lot of responsibility for ceremonies. There are some spiritual Japanese elders who have been channeling the message of extraterrestrials for a long, long time. They are to perform the ceremonies related to opening up a new dimension, asking the Creator to open up a door to this time of purification and the construction of the new world. When we see or hear certain visions or certain things in the sky—whether that is a UFO or a sunbow or rainbow or special shapes of clouds—we know what that means. One person sees a sight; another person dreams of something relating to what that person was shown in the sky; another person may hear something, and it happens that we all call one another to talk about it. We can go to a shrine or to the top of Mount Fuji, our sacred mountain, to ask the Creator for ceremonies to heal the Earth.

Some years ago, certain people created a ceremony to ask the Creator to start the process of ending the old patterns of Earth and opening up the new dimensions. This created a surfacing of purification to cleanse Earth and every being on the planet. We cannot stop the stream of change from flowing. Earth is now moving on to a new dimension, a higher frequency. Our mission is to ask the Creator, through ceremony, to open up the door to that new dimension. Each time we ask, we are shown UFOs or certain symbols in the sky.

The messages from UFOs, and the messages of the ETs all relate to Earth changes and purification; they explain why Earth changes are happening. We can prepare ourselves to know the truth and have love in our heart and in our spirit. The teachings of Meishusama, the practice of Johrei, and nature cultivation become the practical healing methods we can do as human beings. I associate with two circles of people: those who do healing work and those who channel with space brothers and space sisters.

My relationship with the planet Venus is very strong. Many people in America say that they are connected to the Pleiades but my connection is with Venus. This has a lot to do with the teachings of Jesus Christ—not the religious teaching of Christianity, but what Jesus wanted to teach us some two thousand years ago: forgiveness and love. These are the main ingredients of the process of healing. Twelve years ago, I was with a friend in Maine. We were talking about a project when a strong sunbow appeared. It lasted for several hours. During the following seven days, I kept hearing, "Everything has ended. A new beginning." I understood and recognized the change in the new society. The next sunbow I saw was in 1995, and the message was, "Where there is love, there is hope." The latest one came in the late winter of 2001. It was, again, very strong. The sunbow said, "The time is now; now is the time. We are in it." Distractions and constructions are happening at the same time. This is the time of our choice. Do we want to construct a new world? Or do we want to take part in the destruction?

What comes to me throughout my experiences with extraterrestrials and the messages is the word *love*. We can prepare ourselves for the change by having love in our heart and in our spirit. Love is the only thing that we can depend on, isn't it?

THE LORDS OF PALENQUE
by Oscar Rodriguez

World Cycles

World Cycles   Earth Changes   Now Is the Time

A Choice   During   Purification

To Rebuild   Or Destroy   To Be A One-Heart

Or Two-Heart

Sunbow   A Healing   A Message   The Five Colors

Of   A Rainbow   For a Healthy   Body-Mind-Spirit

Cultivate   Compassion   From Dark   To Light

Help Restore   The Planet   Make a Prayer

For Peace   Music   Ceremony   Dance

A Natural Planting   A Vision   Of Love

In Harmony   With the Ancestors

And with Nature

Cooling   The Temperance   Of

A Torid   Wind   Purify

The Fire   The Sky   Will Open

The   Airships

Return   For   The Remnants

Nancy Red Star

Epilogue

Journey of the Star Ancestors

If you have a way to spread the truth, through the newspapers, radio, book, through meetings with powerful people, tell the truth! Tell them what you know to be true. Tell them what you have seen here, what you have heard us say, what you have seen with your own eyes. In this way, if we do fail, let it be said that we tried— right up to the end—to hold fast to the path of peace as we were originally instructed to do by the Great Spirit. Should you really succeed, we will all realize our mistakes of the past and return to the true path: living in harmony as brothers and sisters, sharing our Mother, the Earth, with all other living creatures. In this way, we could bring about a new world.

DAN EVEHENA, ELDEST ELDER,
HOPI SOVEREIGN NATION

My name is Red Star. People will tell you that a red star is not a star at all, but a planet. My message is for this planet from other planets. Stars can take care of themselves.

I have had powerful experiences with other beings. I have been instructed to gather the strands they leave into a powerful rope. Though I am a living testament of a power far greater than I'd ever dreamed of witnessing on an undestroyed Earth—I am not the dispenser of this power. I am a runner. I run from people to people, from old to young, from women to men, from color to color, and from heavens to Earth. I run with a message sent forth from a more advanced race of beings, from other planets. They seek to "wake us up" before we destroy Earth and other planets.

I awoke to my star connection at an early age, with a recurring nightmare that had a powerful impact on my childhood. Some realms need to be revisited; some are seen only once. But again and again, for many years, I would leave my body in bed to travel the cosmos, only to land, in the end, on an earthly soil that seemed to be a "trash can" planet—a backward world strewn with garbage. At the end of the dream there was white, a seamless eternity of white. I understand why I was shown this forecast for the future. Humanity is in the purification, the changing of the cycles and the changing of the guard.

It was soon after the last time I had this dream that I had contact with spacecraft. I was attending the New School of Social Research in New York City, studying film, and I lived in a small flat. It was late one night, and I had just finished up my studies. I went upstairs to where my bed was placed underneath a skylight. The windows were closed and it was dark and cold, but the stars were clearly visible on that October night. I sat on my bed and began to meditate before going to sleep. I had some hand-painted Japanese

INDIAN GIRL
by Tula

glass chimes hanging in the loft. As I was drifting into a closed-eye meditation, in the distance I saw a figure walking toward me. He was almost Christ-like, with long hair and a white robe bound by a gold-twined sash. With each step he took, one hand came forward and opened, and blue morning glory flowers fell from them to the ground. And then the other hand would cross over his chest and more flowers would fall. He kept walking toward me, with this gesture of one hand crossing over the other, and the flowers so beautifully appearing and falling. As he came close, right up in front of my eyes, the Japanese chimes began to ring. They were singing. I opened my eyes and looked up to the skylight. I saw lights—not city lights or moonlight but lights from spacecraft that were moving and dancing in the sky. They seemed to be communicating with each other. A message came through to me; I was told to leave the city, to go to an isolated location in the country.

The next morning I rose very early and caught the train from Grand Central Station to Roxbury, Connecticut. I had a friend there, Aurora, who I knew from art school. I explained to her what had happened. I wanted to have a witness, so I asked her to come with me that night. We walked to a cow pasture at twilight. We stood on the edge of the pasture, then I was intuitively summoned to the middle of the field. I went forward alone and I stood, looking up to the skies. In the distance there were two lights, two craft with beacons transmitting back and forth to each other. Out of nowhere, a third craft emerged, coming toward me with no lights. It passed right over me, just a hundred feet from my head, so that its underside was visible. As it passed overhead I felt a humming, a vibratory frequency with no sound. And then I received another message: "You will be staying here, you have work to do."

What work? I had plans of becoming a professional student or maybe throwing my life to the wind. The message did not make sense to me, and I certainly could not share this experience with many people. So after that, I wandered, with no particular purpose or destination. I traveled to Africa, Asia, Mexico, and all over Europe. I was a runner, but my mailbag was empty. I wasn't delivering anything because I had become a lost soul. I ended up in places that I could not leave. I seemed always to be contemplating how and why I was there, but never looking deep enough within to stop the running. You could say that I was a visitor in the underworld not for a day or a week but for years, occasionally coming up for air only to sink back below the surface. The thoughts of UFOs and extraterrestrials never entered my mind. I was caught up in a survival game, fighting for my life.

In the late 1980s, I had an epiphany, a spiritual experience that changed my life. It was very simple, really. I saw something in someone's eyes—a clarity, a serenity—and I wanted whatever it was for myself. I was spiritually bankrupt, and when I looked in the mirror my eyes reflected back to me only a gray haze, a film of the dead zone. There followed a decision to transform, to regain spirit and possibly return to the path of higher purpose. I could never make the assumption that this decision to change my life was all my own doing. It was far greater than me.

It took more than five years after that spiritual awakening before I was actually able to read again, to complete an entire book. One could say that I had wandered too far off the page. Regaining these abilities to read and write was an exhilarating but painful rebirth for a person who had ended up with all her belongings stuffed in a garbage bag. This is when I began the "Red Road" work, which is a way of life built upon spiritual principles and commitment. Prior to that I had never committed to anything. I was a road woman. So I began to walk the talk, right on into prisons, hospitals, shelters, jails, rehabilitation centers, and universities, carrying a message of experience, strength, and hope. One time I was asked by two brothers who had spent time in Attica to go with them to Sing Sing Prison, a maximum-security facility, to tell my story. The prison was named after the town in which it was built. (The town later changed its name to Ossining.) The town's name of Sing Sing came from the Algonquin phrase "Sin Sinck" that means "stone on stone." The prison is a massive stone building built alongside a granite quarry where the prisoners worked. I was scheduled to be the second speaker. The brother who spoke first was an old flim-flam artist. He talked about how he got by and how he got busted and sent to Attica. The men in the audience were getting very restless and antsy. When my time came to speak, I figured they would start walking out. But nobody moved—all eyes were straight ahead—as I talked about the Red Road and the prayers and Spirit. It seemed as though they really wanted to hear and feel and touch Spirit. Then there was peace. After I spoke, two men came up to me and asked if I would sign their books. They both told me that they were related to Crazy Horse. That was a good day.

I've been on that Good Red Road for fifteen years now, and I never forget where I came from or where I ended up. I lost everything, but in the end I gained my own self, the last thing one can lose. The miracle of it all is that I became who I truly am, a writer. I still, from time to time, look back—but I don't stare.

Around the mid-1990s I had just finished a visiting professorship at a small liberal arts college on the Hudson River, where I had been teaching the course "American Indian Society." My position had been sponsored by the chair of the history department, since I had never had gone to college myself. In fact, I was teaching at the only college I had ever applied to, which had rejected me. The Creator has a great sense of humor! I was on leave and working on an Indian burial repatriation book. One evening, I was at a meeting in Woodstock, New York, and was approached by a producer for the Roswell, New Mexico, fiftieth anniversary music event. U2, Sheryl Crow, Pepsi, and Budweiser were very enthusiastic about it, and sponsorship deals dangled. And Frito-Lay was wild to hit the supermarkets with a UFO corn chip.

I was brought in to film original peoples from all over the world. The footage would be woven into a worldwide satellite link-up and shown on giant monitors during the concert. While doing this work I felt as if my avoidance of a set of instructions, received long ago, had been suddenly terminated. My genetic memories were being activated. The craft didn't come from the skies this time—or not yet, anyway. It came as human craft with the knowledge of the Star

Ancestors. The night before I left Woodstock for Roswell, I had a visit. Around half past five in the morning, I woke up to see three figures standing at the foot of my bed. They were tall, very luminous beings with arms that were crossed over their chest and lotus flowers for hands. These hands emitted light, transmitting it directly into my body. I could not move. Then came a message: "We will not be at Roswell. We will see you in Hopiland." This contact was a long time coming, over twenty years, but at the time it did not make sense to me. I was on my way to Roswell.

But even with pre-production on target and the Hale-Bopp Comet ushering in another cosmic cycle, the grand production was doomed to failure. The Heaven's Gate Cult suicide hit the news and effectively ended any corporate enthusiasm for the Roswell 1997 global music telecast. I had already set out to document indigenous peoples' prophecies of UFOs and extraterrestrials, and the cancellation of the telecast didn't stop me. Many of these prophecies were worldwide, made thousands of years before such terms came to exist. So I gave myself to the road, where the ones you need to find will find you. The unifying theorem—extraterrestrial contact—is here.

PETROGLYPH OF SPACE TRAVEL, ARIZONA

My penultimate encounter began with finding a "talking rock," a small rock with the oval face of a Grey and two large eyes above which, at the crown chakra, rested a telepathic funnel. With this rock I began to pray down our Star Ancestry. My first interview began in the Four Corners at Shiprock, New Mexico. This is an area bordered by four sacred mountains. The Great Shiprock is a natural monolithic structure. This is where the Com Polen deities appeared before Irene Yazzle and set forth a warning: survive by the prayers and the language or the ultimate drought will come to pass. Prophecies say that Four Corners will have a special purpose for the survival of humankind in the future.

The Star Ancestors journey is about a gathering of nations which began at the four corners and extends out to the world to gather the nations, including American Indian, Arab, Israeli, Cuban, Filipino, Australian Aborigine, Celtic, Japanese, Tibetan, and all the world's people. This also includes the extraterrestrials—the Sirians, the Lyrans, the Pleiadians, the Orions, and the Zeta Reticuli. All are represented within every visit. With every interview I receive a teaching to help with my own healing. This includes the extraterrestrials. With every visit, every interview, I receive a teaching to help with my own healing. Not only is the teaching a confirmation of the work being accomplished on the planet at this time, but a greater confirmation of the higher guidance present within a dimension of light and color and sound. We are ascending, and these people who choose to recognize the truths and walk the path share a common purpose.

We are called to take our rightful place in interstellar space—not with weapons of mass destruction, but as human beings following the path of universal laws. These laws have been given to us by higher intelligence through the ages. As I collect teachings from around the world regarding humanity and the Elder races, this is a prophecy fulfilled and this is the mission.

MAYAN SIGNATURE, DEFENDER OF COMMUNITY

Maheyo. Mequich. Great Spirit, Thank You.

Tula Aquila

Illustration Credits

Artist Information

Theresa Bakens
5925 Johnston Drive
Two Rivers, Wisconsin 54241
920-683-9569

Dorit Bat Shalom
Burla 24
Naya, Jerusalem, Israel
Doritdoro@hotmail.com
02-6798117

Desiree Fitzgibbon
The Temenos Studio
P.O. Box 64
Dunally, Tasmania 77, Australia
Painterlydancer@hotmail.com
61-3-62536093

Lenny Foster
Living Light Photography
2464 Ledeux St.
Taos, New Mexico 87529
www.lennyfoster.com
505-737-9150

Mitch Gyson Studios
New York, New York
718-424-7704

Lorne Kris Honyumptewa
P.O. Box 46
Penasco, New Mexico 87553
Lornekrishony@hotmail.com
505-587-0411

Jingalu
Dreamtime Gallery
P.O. Box 1177
Santa Fe, New Mexico 87504
www.dreamtimegallery.com
505-986-0344

Colleen Kelly Studio
6 Frasco Place
Santa Fe, New Mexico 87508
Alivesystems@cybermesa.com
505-466-3960

James Lujan
Taos Productions
Taos Filmmaker's Initiative
Taos, New Mexico 87529
505-758-7859

Athi-Mara Magadi Photography
1954 Hano Rd.
Santa Fe, New Mexico 87505
505-986-0326

Scott Murray Studio
P.O. Box 125
Ranchos de Taos, New Mexico 87557
505-741-0180

Stan Neptune Studio
P.O. Box 128
Old Town, Maine 04468
207-827-6493

Nancy Red Star
and Red Star Productions
In the Spirit of the Drum Institute
PMB 225, 551 Cordova Rd.
Santa Fe, New Mexico 87505
Red@star.mailbox.as
505-776-5038

Oscar Rodriguez
C/o Red Star Productions
PMB 225, 551 Cordova Rd.
Santa Fe, New Mexico 87505
Red@star.mailbox.as

Jerome Water Eagle
P.O. Box 48
Penasco, New Mexico 87553
505-587-2519

Catherine White-Swan Studio
P.O. Box 70315
Houston, Texas 77270
1-800-478-7926

Wings
P.O. Box 328
El Prado, New Mexico 87529
505-776-2555

Books of Related Interest

STAR ANCESTORS
Indian Wisdomkeepers Share the Teachings of the Extraterrestrials
by Nancy Red Star

THE 12TH PLANET
The First Book of The Earth Chronicles
by Zecharia Sitchin

RETURN OF THE CHILDREN OF LIGHT
Incan and Mayan Prophecies for a New World
by Judith Bluestone Polich

BRINGERS OF THE DAWN
Teachings from the Pleiadians
by Barbara Marciniak

FAMILY OF LIGHT
Pleiadian Tales and Lessons in Living
by Barbara Marciniak

THE PLEIADIAN AGENDA
A New Cosmology for the Age of Light
by Barbara Hand Clow

DON JUAN AND THE POWER OF MEDICINE DREAMING
A Nagual Woman's Journey of Healing
by Merilyn Tunneshende

CHOSEN BY THE SPIRITS
Following Your Shamanic Calling
by Sarangerel

Inner Traditions • Bear & Company
P.O. Box 388
Rochester, VT 05767
1-800-246-8648
www.InnerTraditions.com

Or contact your local bookseller